Sweets & Puddings

DAVID & CHARLES

Newton Abbot London

British Library Cataloguing in Publication Data
Sweets & puddings.—(David & Charles Kitchen Workshop)
   1. Desserts.
   I. Desserter. *English*
   641.8'6   TX773

ISBN 0-7153-8456-2

© Illustrations: A/S Hjemmet 1981
   Text: David & Charles 1983

Filmset by MS Filmsetting Limited, Frome, Somerset
and printed in The Netherlands
by Smeets Offset BV, Weert
for David & Charles (Publishers) Limited
Brunel House, Newton Abbot, Devon

Sweets and Puddings

For most busy cooks, everyday meals consist of just a main course and a simple dessert of either fresh fruit or cheese. But at holiday time, on festive occasions and when you are entertaining friends and family, it is nice to serve a mouth-watering dessert. Making delicious desserts is not difficult, but it is often hard to conjure up good ideas. Solve the problem by using the inspiration and advice to be found in the following pages.

Choosing a Dessert

It is important to select a dessert that will be a perfect complement to the other courses of the meal, but particularly the main course. Use your common sense and choose a light dessert such as a sorbet or a dish based on fruit to follow a heavy, filling main course, especially one that is spicy or rich. In a similar way, select more substantial desserts such as pies or crumbles to follow light main courses.

As a general rule, try to avoid using the same major ingredient in both main course and dessert. Do not, for example, serve a cream-based dessert after a main course featuring a cream sauce, or follow roast pork and apple sauce with apple pie. And do not ignore the visual impact of the food you are serving. Choose a dessert whose colours and textures contrast well with those of the main course: thus avoid serving a dark coloured dessert such as a chocolate mousse when a rich beef casserole is on the main course menu.

Cream

In the lists of ingredients for each recipe you will see that three sorts of cream are specified. These are double cream, which has a fat content of about 35 per cent, single cream which contains 20 per cent fat and half cream which is 10 per cent fat. For decoration, whipping cream may be used in place of double cream, but it is important to remember that unlike double cream it does not hold its shape well for long periods. So if you use whipping cream, serve the dessert as soon as possible after it has been prepared.

How to Whip Cream

Cream that is to be whipped should be very cold, and preferably should have been stored in the refrigerator for several hours or overnight. Use a round-bottomed bowl and a pear-shaped wire balloon whisk, a hand-held rotary or electric whisk or the beaters on a food mixer.

With a wire whisk, work from the bottom of the bowl upwards to incorporate as much air as possible into the cream. If you are using a rotary or electric whisk, hold the beaters at a slight angle in the top half of the bowl. If you whisk only at the bottom of the bowl, the cream does not expand as much in volume as it should and is likely to become cheesy. As a rule of thumb, double cream doubles its volume when whipped.

Eggs

It is always essential to use fresh eggs when making desserts. If you are in any doubt about the freshness of eggs, break each one into a cup before you use it to be on the safe side. Eggs vary widely in weight and size. Unless specified, all the recipes in this book call for size 2 or 3 eggs weighing 60–70g (2–2½oz).

Whisking Egg Whites

When the whites of eggs are to be whisked, separate the eggs extremely carefully – even a single drop of yolk in the whites makes it impossible to whisk them stiffly. For the best results, both glass or metal bowl and whisk should be cold, scrupulously clean and free of grease. Egg whites are easiest to whisk when the eggs are used straight from the refrigerator.

Whisk egg whites in the same way as you would whisk cream, working from the bottom of the bowl to trap the maximum amount of air.

After the whites have been whisked they are often folded into a mixture. This is best done with a rubber spatula or a large, shallow metal or wooden spoon. Use a figure of eight motion, going right down to the bottom of the bowl, but never stir the mixture.

Whisking Egg Yolks

Egg yolks should be whisked in the same way as whites, since it is again important to get as much air into the mixture as possible. Whisk egg yolks (and whites) only just before they are needed or the mixture will collapse. When whisked, egg yolksd should have a thick, creamy consistency: you should be able to write your initials on the surface with the whisk.

Gelatine

Gelatine is used to set mousses, jellies and some ice creams. In the recipes given here, powdered gelatine is specified, but gelatine can still be obtained in some places in the old-fashioned leaf form. For the amounts to use, refer to page 14.

Dissolving Gelatine

The secret of success with gelatine is always to sprinkle the powder on to cold water, not the other way round. The gelatine should then be left to soak for 3 to 5 minutes, or until it is spongy, then dissolved over a pan of boiling water before being used in a recipe.

Great care is needed when adding dissolved gelatine to a cold mixture. If it is poured in too quickly it may turn stringy or sink to the bottom of the bowl and form a hard layer. For perfect results every time, work as follows:

Cool the dissolved gelatine a little, stirring in a few teaspoons of hot water if necessary to prevent it becoming thick and lumpy, then pour the gelatine into the cold mixture in a thin, steady stream, whisking or stirring vigorously all the time. Alternatively, pour some of the cold mixture into the dissolved gelatine, stir well, then pour all this into the dessert mixture in a thin stream, whisking or stirring constantly.

For the best finished results, fold fruit, whipped cream or stiffly whisk-ed egg whites into gelatine mixtures only when they are just on the point of setting.

Unmoulding

To turn out a moulded dessert, run a knife around the edge of the mould or loosen the contents with your fingertips. Dip the mould into near-boiling water for a few minutes, place a serving dish on top then turn the mould over, giving it a sharp shake. If you have no success, repeat the operation.

Wines and Spirits

Some of the recipes given here are flavoured with modest amounts of wines and spirits. If you wish they can be replaced by fruit juices or cordials, but the flavour of the finished dish will not be as good.

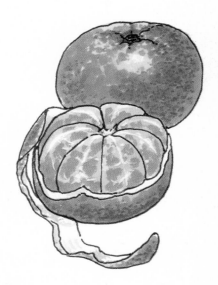

Fluffy Mousses

Mousses are favourites with all the family. The method and ingredients for mousse making are nearly always the same – it is the flavours that vary. Mocha and nut mousses are good dinner-party desserts while orange, chocolate and banana mousses are especially popular with children.

Mocha Mousse (left)
(serves 4–6)
Preparation time: about 20 min
Setting time: 3–4 hr
Suitable for the freezer

15g (½oz) gelatine
4 egg yolks
85g (3½oz) caster sugar
250ml (9fl oz) milk
1 × 15ml tbsp (1tbsp) instant coffee
1 × 5ml tsp (1tsp) cocoa
250ml (9fl oz) double cream
50–100g (2–4oz) chocolate beans or drops

1 Sprinkle gelatine over 2–3 × 15ml tbsp (2–3tbsp) cold water and leave to soak for 5 min. Whisk egg yolks with sugar until fluffy.
2 Bring milk, instant coffee and cocoa to the boil. Whisk boiling milk into the whisked egg yolks. Pour mixture back into saucepan and whisk, without boiling, until cream thickens.

3 Add gelatine mixture to warm cream. Stir well until gelatine has dissolved completely and mix well with the cream. Cool for a few minutes until cream starts to stiffen.
4 Whip cream until standing in soft peaks and fold into egg custard. Rinse a ring mould with cold water and pour in mousse mixture. Cover with foil or cling film and cool in refrigerator.
5 When mousse has set, run a knife around the edge then dip mould in boiling water for 3–4 sec and unmould mousse onto a serving dish. If it does not come out first time, dip it in hot water again.
Decorate with chocolate beans or buttons before serving.

Nut Mousse (below)
(serves 4–6)
Preparation time: 25–30 min
Setting time: about 2 hr
Suitable for the freezer without the raspberries

15g (½oz) gelatine
4 eggs
50g (2oz) caster sugar
100ml (4fl oz) sweet sherry
50g (2oz) plain cooking chocolate
50–75g (2–3oz) chopped hazelnuts or walnuts
250ml (9fl oz) double cream
about 300g (11oz) fresh or defrosted frozen raspberries

1 Sprinkle gelatine over 2–3 × 15ml tbsp (2–3tbsp) cold water. Whisk egg yolks with sugar until very stiff then fold in coarsely grated or chopped chocolate and nuts.

2 Dissolve gelatine over a saucepan of boiling water. It should *not* be allowed to boil. Mix in the sherry and stir into whisked egg yolks.
3 Whisk egg whites and cream separately until standing in stiff peaks. Carefully fold into whisked egg yolks. Rinse a ring mould in cold water and pour in mousse mixture. Cover with foil and refrigerate until mousse is set.
4 Pick over fresh raspberries and rinse carefully if necessary. Defrost frozen fruit in a colander with a bowl underneath (you can either drink the juice or use it in other desserts). To unmould, dip mould in very hot water for a moment then turn out onto a serving dish. Fill the centre with raspberries.
Serve cold accompanied by a glass of sherry of the same kind as used in the dessert.

Lemon Mousse
(serves 6)
Preparation time: about 15 min
Setting time: about 2 hr
Suitable for the freezer without decoration

15g (½oz) gelatine
5–6 eggs
85g (3½oz) caster sugar
3 lemons
300–400ml (½–¾pt) double cream

1 Sprinkle gelatine over 2–3 × 15ml tbsp (2–3tbsp) cold water in a heatproof bowl. Scrub 1 lemon well under tepid water with a stiff brush.

(cont)

Rinse with cold water and dry well. Grate zest finely. Squeeze juice from all lemons.

2 Whisk egg yolks with sugar until fluffy. Dissolve gelatine over a-saucepan of boiling water. Add lemon juice and dissolve whisked egg yolks with 2–3 × 5ml tsp (2–3tsp) grated lemon zest.

3 Whisk egg whites and cream separately until standing in stiff peaks. Fold egg whites and about half the cream into the whisked egg yolks. Pour into a glass bowl and leave in a cold place until set. Serve decorated with whipped cream and grated lemon zest as decoration.

Almond-rice Mousse
(serves 4)
Preparation time: about 20 min
Setting time: 1–2 hr
Suitable for the freezer

10g ($\frac{1}{3}$oz) gelatine
2 eggs
40g (1$\frac{3}{4}$oz) caster sugar
50–75g (2–3oz) almonds
a few drops of vanilla essence
about 200ml (7fl oz) cold rice
*   pudding*
250ml (9fl oz) double cream

1 Sprinkle gelatine over 2–3 × 15ml tbsp (2–3tbsp) cold water in a heat-proof bowl. Whisk egg yolks with sugar until thick. Blanch the almonds. Cut half into flakes or chop roughly and grind the remainder or chop them finely. Mix ground almonds with whisked egg yolks and vanilla essence.

2 Dissolve gelatine over a saucepan of boiling water and fold into whisked egg yolks with the cold rice pudding. Whisk egg whites until standing in stiff peaks and whisk cream until standing in soft peaks. Carefully fold egg whites and cream into the egg and rice mixture. Stir occasionally during setting.

3 Toast almonds under the grill until golden and sprinkle over dessert. Serve this mousse cold with cold or warm cherry sauce.

Cherry Sauce
Heat a large can of sweet cherries or 300ml ($\frac{1}{2}$pt) sweet cherry juice until nearly boiling then thicken with 2 × 5ml tsp (2tsp) cornflour dissolved in 3 × 15ml tbsp (3tbsp) water. Bring to the boil and pour into a jug. Sprinkle with a little sugar. Serve sauce cold or warm.

Ideal for a dinner party – Sherry Mousse decorated with chopped nuts and chocolate and lightly whipped cream.

Sherry Mousse
(serves 4)
Preparation time: about 15 min
Setting time: 1–2 hr
Suitable for the freezer without decoration

15g ($\frac{1}{2}$oz) gelatine
1 egg
2 egg yolks
4 × 15ml tbsp (4tbsp) caster sugar
150ml ($\frac{1}{4}$pt) sweet sherry
50ml (2fl oz) double cream
50g (2oz) plain cooking chocolate
25g (1oz) walnuts
*   or 2 × 15ml tbsp (2tbsp) sherry*

1 Sprinkle gelatine over 2–3 × 15ml tbsp (2–3tbsp) cold water in a heat-proof bowl. Whisk 1 whole egg and egg yolks with sugar until stiff. Add 1 × 15ml tbsp (1tbsp) boiling water to gelatine and dissolve over a saucepan of boiling water. Mix in sherry.

2 Whisk cream until standing in soft peaks. Remove $\frac{1}{3}$ of the cream

Try Almond-rice Mousse with Cherry Sauce if you have some rice pudding left over.

Banana Mousse with sautéed nuts is served in individual ramekins.

and set aside in the refrigerator.

3 Mix gelatine and sherry mixture into whisked egg yolks and stir occasionally, until mousse starts to set. Carefully fold $\frac{2}{3}$ of cream into whisked egg yolk mixture and pour into a ring mould rinsed with cold water. Set aside in a cool place.

4 Turn mousse out onto a dish (see Mocha Mousse, page 7) and sprinkle with more sherry if necessary. Pile the rest of the cream into the centre and decorate with coarsely chopped chocolate and nuts.
Serve cold.

Port Mousse

Follow the method for Sherry Mousse, but use a medium port.

Rum Mousse

See page 17.

Banana Mousse

(serves 4)
Preparation time: about 20 min
Setting time: 1–2 hr
Unsuitable for the freezer

10g (⅓oz) gelatine
2 eggs
85g (3½oz) caster sugar
4 bananas
1–2 lemons
50–75g (2–3oz) cooking chocolate
250ml (9fl oz) double cream
50g (2oz) hazelnuts

1 Sprinkle gelatine over 2 × 15ml tbsp (2tbsp) cold water in a heat-proof bowl. Whisk egg yolks and sugar until thick. Peel bananas and pass through a sieve or work in a blender with lemon juice. Add lemon juice immediately to avoid discoloration. Whisk bananas until foamy and fold into whisked yolks.

2 Dissolve gelatine over a saucepan of boiling water. Mix with banana and egg mixture along with chopped chocolate and 1–2 × 5ml tsp (1–2tsp) finely grated lemon zest.

3 Whisk egg whites and cream separately until standing in stiff peaks. Fold into banana and egg mixture. Cut out 4 strips of greaseproof paper and brush with oil. Tie around the top edges of small individual soufflé dishes to come 1–2cm (½–¾in) above the top. Fasten with paper clips. Pour in mixture.

4 Refrigerate until set and remove paper strips. Chop the nuts coarsely, brown under the grill and sprinkle over mousse.
Serve cold with a glass of port or medium sherry.

Creamy Chocolate Mousse
(above)
(serves 4)
Preparation time: about 15 min
Setting time: 2–3 hr
Suitable for the freezer without
decoration

15g (½oz) gelatine
1 egg
2 egg yolks
4 × 15ml tbsp (4tbsp) caster sugar
100g (4oz) cooking chocolate
200ml (7fl oz) milk or single cream
1 × 15ml tbsp (1tbsp) brandy
  (optional)
250ml (9fl oz) double cream

1 Sprinkle gelatine over 2–3 × 15ml
tbsp (2–3tbsp) cold water in a heat-
proof bowl. Whisk egg and egg yolks
with sugar until fluffy. Break 75g
(3oz) chocolate into small pieces and
melt in warm milk or cream over low
heat. Dissolve gelatine over boiling
water, adding chocolate milk mix-

ture. Leave to cool for a while.
2 Add brandy, if using, then stir
chocolate milk mixture into whisked
egg yolks and refrigerate until on the
point of setting. Whisk cream and
fold most of it carefully into mousse.
Pile into glasses and refrigerate.
3 Decorate with a rosette of whipped cream and grated chocolate.

Dark Chocolate Mousse
(serves 4)
Preparation time: about 15 min
Setting time: 1–2 hr
Unsuitable for the freezer

100g (4oz) plain cooking chocolate
2 × 15ml tbsp (2tbsp) caster sugar
4 egg yolks
1 × 15ml tbsp (1tbsp) rum or brandy
250ml (9fl oz) double cream
25g (1oz) almonds

1 Break chocolate into small pieces
and place in a heatproof bowl. Melt
over a saucepan of hot, but not boil-

ing water, stirring carefully until
chocolate melts.
2 Whisk egg yolks and sugar until
fluffy then stir in rum or brandy and
melted, slightly cooled chocolate.
3 Whip cream until standing in soft
peaks. Fold most of the cream into
the egg mixture. Divide mousse
mixture between individual glasses
and refrigerate. Decorate with a rosette of cream and blanched, chopped
almonds just before serving.

Layered Cream Mousse
(serves 4)
Preparation time: about 20 min
Setting time: 1–2 hr
Suitable for the freezer without
decoration

15g (½oz) gelatine
500ml (about 1 pt) double cream
1 × 15ml tbsp (1tbsp) caster sugar
several drops of vanilla essence
50g (2oz) plain cooking chocolate
2 × 5ml tsp (2tsp) instant coffee

*1 × 5ml tsp (1tsp) cocoa
4 maraschino cherries*

1 Break chocolate into small pieces
and melt over a saucepan of hot
water. Dissolve instant coffee and
cocoa in 1 × 15ml tbsp (1tbsp) boiling water or cream. Leave to cool.
2 Sprinkle gelatine over 4 × 15ml
tbsp (4tbsp) cold water then dissolve
over boiling water. Whip cream
until nearly stiff and remove about
100ml (4fl oz). Set this aside in
the refrigerator. Season remaining
cream with sugar and vanilla and
mix in gelatine.
3 Divide into three parts. Stir the
melted chocolate into one, the dissolved instant coffee and cocoa into
another and the third unflavoured.
4 When the mixtures are nearly set,
spoon in layers into individual
glasses, then refrigerate. Decorate
with piped cream and maraschino
cherries before serving.

Pineapple Mousse
(serves 4)
Preparation time: about 20 min
Setting time: 1–2 hr
Suitable for the freezer without
decoration

*15g (½oz) gelatine
2 eggs
40g (1¾oz) caster sugar
1 small can pineapple
juice of 1 lemon
250ml (9fl oz) double cream
25g (1oz) almonds
a few maraschino cherries (optional)*

1 Sprinkle gelatine over 2–3 × 15ml
tbsp (2–3tbsp) cold water in a heat-
proof bowl. Whisk egg yolks and
sugar until fluffy. Add about 100ml
(4fl oz) pineapple juice to gelatine
then dissolve over a pan of boiling
water. Mix in lemon juice then stir
into egg mixture.
2 Chop pineapple finely and fold
into egg mixture once it starts to set.
Whisk egg whites until standing in
stiff peaks and whip cream. Fold in
egg whites and cream.
3 Pour mousse mixture into individual glasses and refrigerate.
Blanch and flake almonds, then grill
lightly to brown. Decorate each
mousse with a spoonful of cream,
almond flakes and a cherry.

Below : Coffee Liqueur Mousse (see overleaf).

Cream Mousse with Brandied Oranges – the perfect dessert to follow a light main course.

Coffee Liqueur Mousse

(serves 4)
Preparation time: about 20 min
Setting time: 2–3 hr
Unsuitable for the freezer

85g (3½oz) caster sugar
100ml (4fl oz) water
2 eggs
150g (5oz) plain cooking chocolate
3–4 × 15ml tbsp (3–4tbsp) coffee
   liqueur (eg Tia Maria)
250ml (9fl oz) double cream
crystallized violets or other cake
   decorations

1 Put sugar and water in a saucepan and boil until volume is reduced by about half.
2 Whisk eggs with finely grated chocolate until thick and fluffy. Add sugar syrup and coffee liqueur, a little at a time, whisking constantly. Set aside to cool.
3 Whip the cream and carefully fold into chocolate cream. Divide between 4 individual ramekins or soufflé dishes and refrigerate until set. Decorate with crystallized violets.

Cream Mousse with Brandied Oranges

(serves 4–5)
Preparation time: about 20 min
Cooling time: 2–3 hr
Suitable for the freezer without oranges

2 thick-skinned oranges
100ml (4fl oz) water
juice of ½ lemon
8 × 15ml tbsp (8tbsp) caster sugar
2½ × 15ml tbsp (2½tbsp) brandy
8g (¼oz) gelatine
2 eggs
2 egg yolks
300ml (½pt) single cream
250ml (9fl oz) double cream

1 Scrub oranges with a brush, rinse well and cut into wafer thin slices. Parboil orange slices for about 5 min in water with 4 × 15ml tbsp (4tbsp) sugar and 1–2 × 15ml tbsp (1–2tbsp) lemon juice added. Remove saucepan from heat and mix in brandy. Cool oranges in syrup.
2 Sprinkle gelatine over 2 × 15ml tbsp (2tbsp) cold water. Whisk whole eggs and egg yolks with sugar until thick. Bring single cream to the boil and pour into egg mixture while still boiling hot, whisking vigorously. Dissolve gelatine over boiling

water and add to the warm mixture. Stir well.
3 Add syrup from oranges and stir from time to time, until cream starts to thicken. Whisk double cream until nearly stiff and fold carefully into mousse with most of the orange slices. Pour mixture into a bowl and place the remaining orange slices on top. Serve soufflé cool, but not chilled.

Classic Vanilla Mousse

1 Place bowl containing egg mixture over a pan of hot water. Stir until cream thickly coats back of spoon.

Classic Vanilla Mousse (right)
(Crème Bavarois)

(serves 4–6)
Preparation time: about 20 min
Setting time: 2–3 hr
Suitable for the freezer without
decoration

15g (½oz) gelatine
4 egg yolks
6 × 15ml tbsp (6tbsp) caster sugar
250ml (9fl oz) milk
1 vanilla pod
300–400ml (½–¾pt) double cream
maraschino cherries, flaked almonds

1 Sprinkle gelatine over 3 × 15ml
tbsp (3tbsp) cold water. In a heat-
proof bowl, whisk egg yolks with
sugar until fluffy and add milk a
little at a time. Slice vanilla pod,
scrape out seeds and stir into egg
mixture.

2 Place bowl over a pan of very hot
water and stir constantly until cream
is thick and smooth. Dissolve gelatine over boiling water and add to
thickened cream, stirring. Set thickened cream aside and cool, stirring
from time to time.

3 Whip double cream until thick
and fold about ⅔ of it into the cream
mixture. Rinse 4 individual moulds
in cold water and divide mousse
mixture between them. Refrigerate
until set.

4 Dip moulds into hot water, one at
a time, and turn out onto individual
dishes. Decorate with remaining
cream, maraschino cherries and
toasted almond flakes.

Serve well chilled accompanied by a
glass of medium sherry.

*2 Whisk cream until stiff (it should be
thicker than for an ordinary mousse).*

*3 Mix the whipped cream into egg
mixture and beat until well mixed.*

*4 Unmould mousses by running a
knife around the edge then dipping
moulds in hot water.*

Jellies

Jellies are made of fruit juice, wine or any other flavoured liquid set with gelatine. Most gelatine is now sold in powdered form, but traditional leaves or sheets are still available in some places. The amount of gelatine you need depends on the dessert you are making. For a jelly that is to be unmoulded you need 15–20g ($\frac{1}{2}$–$\frac{3}{4}$oz) powdered gelatine or 8–9 leaves per 500ml (1pt) liquid. For jellies served in individual glasses a scant 15g ($\frac{1}{2}$oz) or 5–6 leaves is sufficient to set the same amount of liquid.

If the jelly is being used as a glaze, only 8–10g ($\frac{1}{4}$–$\frac{1}{3}$oz) gelatine or 4 leaves is needed per 500ml (1pt).

Red Wine Jelly (left)
(serves 4)
Preparation time: 15–20 min
Setting time: at least 2–3 hr
Unsuitable for the freezer

50g (2oz) raisins
3–4 lemons
2–3 × 15ml tbsp (2–3tbsp) caster
* sugar*
generous 15g ($\frac{1}{2}$oz) gelatine
500ml (1pt) rosé or red wine
2 × 15ml tbsp (2tbsp) raspberry
* liqueur or concentrated raspberry*
* juice*
100–200ml (4–7fl oz) double cream
brown sugar

1 Soak raisins in juice of 1 lemon mixed with sugar. Sprinkle gelatine over 2–3 × 15ml tbsp (2–3tbsp) cold water. Peel the remaining lemons and remove all the pith. Divide into segments, pull off the membranes on each and chop. Divide lemons and raisins between 4 individual glasses.
2 Heat the wine, but do not allow to boil. Dissolve gelatine over boiling water and add to wine. Mix in raspberry liqueur or juice. Pour into individual glasses and refrigerate until set.
3 Decorate each serving with a rosette of whipped cream and sprinkle with a little brown sugar.

Glazed Strawberry Cake
(serves 6)
Preparation time: about 15 min
Setting time: 1–2 hr
Unsuitable for the freezer

Dissolving Gelatine
1 Soak gelatine leaves in or sprinkle powder over cold water.

2. Put gelatine into a bowl, with fruit juice, if you wish. Dissolve over a saucepan of boiling water.

500g (1lb 2oz) fresh strawberries
sugar
1 sponge cake, either home or ready
    made
vanilla custard
8g (¼oz) gelatine
300ml (½pt) strawberry juice
2–3 × 15ml tbsp (2–3tbsp) sherry

1 Wash and hull strawberries and rinse if necessary. Sprinkle with sugar.
2 Sprinkle sponge cake base with a little juice from strawberries and a little sherry and leave for about 1 hr.
3 Sprinkle gelatine over 2 × 15ml tbsp (2tbsp) cold water in a heat-proof bowl. Heat strawberry juice, but do not allow to boil. Add to gelatine and heat over boiling water until gelatine has dissolved. Stir in sherry. Leave jelly in a cold place until nearly set.
4 Spread custard over cake and arrange strawberries on top. Carefully spoon jelly over, until all the fruit is covered. Leave cake in a cool place until jelly is completely set. Serve cake with cold, whipped cream, soured cream or vanilla ice cream.

Orange Jelly
(serves 4–5)
Preparation time: about 15 min
Setting time: at least 2–3 hr
Unsuitable for the freezer

25g (1oz) gelatine
150g (5oz) caster sugar
250ml (9fl oz) water
5–6 large oranges
1–2 lemons
100–200ml (4–7fl oz) double cream
grated chocolate

1 Sprinkle gelatine over 100ml (4fl oz) cold water. Make a syrup of sugar and remaining water, add gelatine and dissolve over hot water.
2 Squeeze oranges and lemons and strain juice through a fine-meshed sieve into sugar syrup. Pour jelly into individual glasses and leave in a cold place until set.
3 Decorate with cream and grated chocolate.

Above right: Glazed Strawberry Cake. Right: Fresh, tangy Orange Jelly.

Grapes in Wine Jelly

1 Make sure all grape halves are placed in ring mould with the rounded side facing downwards. This will make the dessert look as if it has been made with whole grapes.

2 Pour a thin layer of jelly over each layer of grapes and leave to set, before adding more grapes to ring tin. Make sure the remaining jelly stays half set until the last layer of grapes has been completely covered.

Grapes in Wine Jelly
(serves 6–8)
Preparation time: about 20 min
Setting time: at least 1–2 hr
Unsuitable for the freezer

40g (1½oz) gelatine
700g–1kg (1½–2¼lb) grapes
85g (3½oz) sugar
250ml (9fl oz) water
½ lemon
1 × 700–750ml (about 1¼pt) bottle white wine

1 Sprinkle gelatine over half the water. Rinse grapes and dry thoroughly on absorbent paper. Halve and remove pips.
2 Make a syrup of sugar, remaining water, lemon juice and wine. Add soaked gelatine and dissolve over a pan of boiling water, stirring.
3 Rinse out a 1½litre (2½pt) ring mould with cold water. Pour in 1cm (about ½in) jelly into mould. Turn mould slowly so that jelly is distributed well up the sides. Place halved grapes in mould with rounded sides facing downwards. Continue adding jelly and grapes as shown in small illustrations.
4 Cover mould with foil and refrigerate overnight. Loosen jelly around the eges with a sharp knife, dip mould in very hot water for 3 seconds. Place a dish on top of mould and turn out. Fill the centre with whipped cream either unflavoured or with a little port wine and sifted icing sugar added. If 1 × 5ml tsp (1tsp) dissolved gelatine is added to the cream with the port it will not collapse when whipped and can be prepared well in advance.

Left: Grapes in Wine Jelly is a dessert which will call for compliments. Easy to make, it is just as delicious as it looks.

Right: Three delicious desserts. From the left: Peaches in Jelly, Lemon Sorbet (see page 18) and Rum Mousse with Lemon Jelly.

Peaches in Jelly

(serves 4–5)
Preparation time: about 20 min
Setting time: at least 2–3 hr
Unsuitable for the freezer

15g (½oz) gelatine
3–4 oranges
1 can peach halves
Vanilla cream:
2 egg yolks
2–3 × 15ml tbsp (2–3tbsp) caster sugar
1 × 5ml tsp (1tsp) vanilla sugar
250ml (9fl oz) double cream

1 Sprinkle gelatine over 4 × 15ml tbsp (4tbsp) cold water in a heat-proof bowl. Squeeze oranges and mix juice with syrup from peaches to make 500ml (1pt) juice in all.
2 Dissolve gelatine over boiling water. Pour slowly into fruit juice and stir well.
3 Rinse 4–5 glasses with cold water. Pour in 1–2cm (½–¾in) jelly. Refrigerate until set, but leave re-maining jelly at room temperature so it stays semi-liquid.
4 Place a well-drained peach in each glass, round-side downwards, and pour jelly carefully over peach until it is completely covered. Return glasses to refrigerator. When jelly is set, dip them into near-boiling water and unmould.
Serve jelly with vanilla cream: whisk egg yolks, vanilla sugar and sugar until foamy and fold into whipped cream.

Rum Mousse with Lemon Jelly

(serves 4)
Preparation time: 20–25 min
Cooling time: at least 2–3 hr
Suitable for the freezer without jelly

scant 15g (½oz) gelatine
4 egg yolks
6 × 15ml tbsp (6tbsp) caster sugar
100–150ml (4–5fl oz) white rum
3 egg whites
500ml (1pt) double cream

For the jelly:
8g (¼oz) gelatine
100ml (4fl oz) water
juice of 1 lemon
40g (1½oz) sugar

1 First make mousse: sprinkle ge-latine over 3 × 15ml tbsp (3tbsp) cold water. Whisk egg yolks with sugar until fluffy. Dissolve gelatine over a pan of boiling water. Stir in rum and add to egg mixture.
2 Whisk egg whites until standing in stiff peaks. Whip the cream. Set aside ⅓ of cream, cover with foil and refrigerate. Fold egg whites into egg mixture then fold in ⅔ of cream. Pour into a bowl and refrigerate until set.
3 Sprinkle gelatine for jelly over 2 × 15ml tbsp (2tbsp) cold water. Make a sugar syrup from sugar, remaining water and lemon juice. Add gelatine and dissolve over a pan of boiling water. When jelly is thick but not set pour carefully over rum mousse. Chill until jelly is set.

Sorbets

These deliciously fresh-tasting frozen desserts, often also called water ices, are made from fruit juice or purée and sugar syrup, often with wine or liqueur added. This mixture is then frozen, during which time it is whisked frequently. Stiffly whisked egg white may be added for extra lightness.

Sugar Syrup

The amount of sugar must not exceed 600–700g (1¼–1½lb) per 500ml (1pt) water or the sorbet will not solidify. When using sweetened fruit juice or juice from puréed fruit which has been sprinkled with sugar, the syrup should contain less sugar to taste.

Equipment

An electric juice extractor and/or a blender are handy for making sorbets from fresh fruit. An ordinary lemon squeezer is, however, perfectly adequate for making orange and lemon sorbets, or you can buy ready-prepared fruit juice.

Freezing

Fruit juice or thin purée is poured into a rigid freezerproof container with a tightly fitting lid. Because it is always easier to whisk in rounded utensils and metal is a better conductor of heat than plastic, for preference use a metal bowl. Freezing takes 2–6 hr. A sorbet with a high sugar content and with any sort of alcohol added takes longer to freeze. During freezing the sorbet must be whisked 3 or 4 times with a hand-held whisk. It is ready when it is solid but not hard, and should have a light, fluffy consistency. If the sorbet is not to be used within a few days, add a lightly whisked egg white when the sorbet is nearly solid to extend the keeping time.

Serving

Whisk the sorbet quickly until it has a firm consistency. Using a spoon dipped in tepid water, transfer it to chilled individual glasses. (Leave them in the refrigerator for a few hours before serving or the sorbet will melt too quickly.) Make sure any decorations are to hand, then decorate and serve immediately.

Melon Sorbet
(serves 4)

about 300g (11oz) melon flesh
150g (5oz) sugar
100ml (4fl oz) water
1–2 × 15ml tbsp (1–2tbsp) preserved ginger
1 × 15ml tbsp (1tbsp) syrup from preserved ginger
50–100ml (2–4fl oz) white wine
artificial colouring (optional)

Make a syrup from the sugar and water. Cool. Pour all the ingredients into the goblet of a blender and work to a smooth thin purée. Freeze, whisking from time to time as in basic method. Serve undecorated.

Kiwi Sorbet
(serves 4)

about 450g (1lb) ripe kiwi fruit
125g (4½oz) sugar
150ml (¼pt) water
juice of ½–1 lemon

Peel kiwi fruit and place in blender goblet with cooled sugar syrup. Work for a few seconds to give a thin purée. Flavour to taste with lemon juice, freeze and whisk as in basic method. Serve undecorated.

Lemon Sorbet
(serves 5–6)

4–6 lemons
225g (8oz) sugar
400ml (¾pt) water
250ml (9fl oz) double cream
maraschino cherries

Squeeze 4–6 lemons, strain juice and mix with well chilled sugar syrup. Increase sugar content in brine to 350–400g (12–14oz) if wished, but lemon sorbet should have a tangy, acid flavour. Freeze and whisk as in basic method. Lemon sorbet can be seasoned with white vermouth.

Orange Sorbet

Follow the recipe for Lemon Sorbet, but use the smaller amount of sugar in the syrup.

Champagne Sorbet

(serves 6–8)

400–500ml (¾–1pt) medium dry champagne or sparkling white wine
1 orange
1 lemon
225g (8oz) sugar
200ml (7fl oz) water
300–400ml (½–¾pt) unsweetened mineral water
crystallized violets or other decoration

Make a syrup of sugar and water and cool. Squeeze juice from orange and lemon. Mix all liquid ingredients and freeze, whisking from time to time. Sprinkle with crystallized violets or other cake decorations before serving.

Blackberry or Raspberry Sorbet

(serves 4)

500ml (1pt) slightly sweetened blackberry or raspberry juice
150g (5oz) sugar
100ml (4fl oz) water
juice of ½–1 lemon

If you use shop bought juice, the syrup should be made with less sugar. Mix juice with cooled sugar syrup and flavour. Freeze and whisk as in basic method and serve undecorated.

Sorbet

1 Make a sugar syrup. Squeeze juice from fruit and add to syrup.

A row of fresh, light sorbets. From the left: Melon, Champagne, Kiwi Fruit and Blackberry Sorbets.

Blackcurrant Sorbet

Follow the recipe for Blackberry Sorbet but use homemade or bought blackcurrant juice. Flavour with rum if you wish.

2 Freeze, whisking several times during freezing. Fold in a stiffly whisked egg white when sorbet is half frozen to extend keeping time.

Dessert Gâteaux

A delicious dessert gâteau makes a perfect accompaniment for a cup of coffee after a meal.

Marzipan Tart

(serves 8–10)
Preparation time: about 1 hr
Round flan tin, about 22cm (9in) diameter
Baking time: about 10 min
Oven temperature (middle shelf): 200–225°C, 400–425°F, Gas 6–7
Suitable for the freezer without filling

500g (1lb 2oz) ground almonds
225g (8oz) icing sugar
3–4 egg whites
150g (5oz) cooking chocolate
½ × 15ml tbsp (½tbsp) vegetable oil
500ml (1pt) double cream
4 × 15ml tbsp (4tbsp) coffee or other liqueur
1 can figs or pears (optional)
1 can mandarin orange segments
small can pineapple rings

1 Mix ground almonds with sifted icing sugar. Knead in egg whites, a little at a time, to give a stiff dough. Transfer to a heavy-based saucepan and cook over low heat, stirring all the time, until mixture is smooth and soft enough to be piped.
2 Grease and flour tin. Spread about half the marzipan mixture over the base of the tin in an even layer. Spoon the remaining mixture into a piping bag with a fairly large star nozzle. Pipe round the outer edge of the dough then pipe small rosettes on a baking sheet covered with baking parchment.
3 Bake rosettes in preheated oven for 7–8 min and cake base for 10 min. The edge of the base can be covered with greaseproof paper if it is browning too quickly. Cool base and rosettes. Place base on a serving dish.
4 Melt chocolate in a bowl over a saucepan of boiling water, mix in vegetable oil. Brush ¾ of the chocolate over cake base. Pour canned fruit into a sieve and drain well. Cut pineapple, and figs or pears, into pieces. Whip cream and flavour with liqueur. Place fruit and cream in layers in cake base, to form a pyramid (see photograph). Decorate with rosettes and melted chocolate.

Rubenstein Gâteau

(serves 8–10)
Preparation time: 1 hr 15 min
Baking time, almond base: about 15 min
Baking time, petits choux: about 30 min
Oven temperature (middle shelf): 150 and 200°C, 300 and 400°F, Gas 2 and 6
Almond base, rum soufflé and petits choux can all be frozen separately

For the almond base :
100g (4oz) ground almonds
2 egg whites
100g (4oz) caster sugar
¼ × 5ml tsp (¼tsp) bicarbonate of soda
100–150ml (4–5fl oz) rum
500g (1lb 2oz) raspberries, frozen and defrosted, or fresh
sugar
For the mousse :
4 egg yolks
4 × 15ml tbsp (4tbsp) caster sugar
15g (½oz) gelatine
3 egg whites
250ml (9fl oz) double cream
For the petits choux :
100ml (4fl oz) water
50g (2oz) butter
60g (2½oz) plain flour
2 eggs
250ml (9fl oz) double cream
100g (4oz) cooking chocolate
1 × 5ml tsp (1tsp) oil

1 In a saucepan, mix almonds, egg whites and sugar. Cook over low heat, stirring all the time, until the mixture is smooth. Dissolve bicarbonate of soda in 2 × 5ml tsp (2tsp) water and stir into almond mixture. Mark a circle of about 20cm (8in) diameter on baking parchment. Spread mixture evenly within circle and bake for 15 min at 150°C, 300°F, Gas 2. Cool.
2 Make the mousse: whisk egg yolks and sugar until fluffy. Add 50–100ml (2–4fl oz) rum and soaked, dissolved gelatine. Whisk egg whites until standing in stiff peaks and whip cream. Carefully fold egg whites and cream into whisked egg yolks and sugar. Select a bowl with a diameter a little less than cake base and rinse in cold water. Pour in mousse mixture and refrigerate until set.
3 Make the petits choux: put the water and butter in a saucepan and bring to the boil. Add the flour all at once and stir vigorously until dough leaves the sides of the pan easily. Remove pan from heat and beat in eggs, one at a time, to give a stiff dough. Pipe or spoon small amounts of dough onto a baking sheet with a piping bag or teaspoon. Bake as indicated above but do not open oven door for the first 20 min. Cool petits choux and cut 10–12 of them in half (freeze the rest). Melt chocolate in a bowl over a saucepan of boiling water, add 1 × 5ml tsp oil. Fill petits choux with whipped cream and coat with chocolate.
4 Place almond base on a serving dish and sprinkle with the remaining rum. Mash half the raspberries, sprinkle with sugar and spread purée over cake base. Turn soufflé out on to the middle of the cake base and arrange petits choux around the edge. Decorate with the remaining raspberries.

Rubenstein Gâteau is a classic. It takes considerable time to make, but is well worth every minute!

Left : Marzipan Tart – a dessert for a grand occasion.

Above: Savarins, like this one shown filled with ice cream and caramel sauce, can be baked in individual moulds. Below: Strawberry Savarin looks especially grand when glazed with a sugar syrup mixed with a little redcurrant jelly.

Savarins

A savarin is a French dessert cake made from yeast dough. It is baked in a ring mould and sprinkled with hot sugar syrup with rum, brandy, wine and/or fruit juice added.

Savarin (basic recipe)
Preparation time: 30–40 min
Rising time: about 40 min
Ring mould: about 1½litres (2½pt)
Baking time: 25–30 min
Oven temperature (bottom shelf):
200°C, 400°F, Gas 6
Standing time: about 3 hr
Unsuitable for the freezer

For the dough:
150g (5oz) butter
100ml (4fl oz) milk or half cream
25g (1oz) yeast
½ × 5ml tsp (½tsp) salt
1 × 15ml tbsp (1tbsp) caster sugar
3 eggs
about 200g (7oz) plain flour
For the syrup:
300ml (½pt) water
200g (7oz) sugar
75–100ml (3–4fl oz) rum or brandy
or 150ml (¼pt) wine or fruit juice
(see individual recipes)

1 Melt the butter, mix in milk or cream and allow mixture to cool. Dissolve yeast in warm milk and set aside for about 20 min until frothy. Add salt, sugar, whisked eggs and flour. Knead dough until smooth and shiny, cover and leave in a warm place for about 40 min until well risen.
2 Knock down the dough and place in a well greased and floured ring mould. Bake as indicated until a wooden cocktail stick inserted in the cake comes out clean.
Leave cake in the mould for a while, then turn out onto a wire rack to cool. Wash mould and carefully replace cake in it.
3 Make a syrup of water and sugar and boil uncovered for about 20 min until thick, but not for so long that the sugar crystallizes. Cool for a while, then stir in flavouring ingredients.
4 Prick the cake very thoroughly all over with a knitting needle.

Gradually spoon over the sugar syrup, allowing the cake to soak up liquid between each addition. Leave cake to stand for a total of 3 hr. After about half this time, turn out on to a serving dish, so that the syrup which has accumulated at the bottom can be incorporated.

Fill the cake with fruit or other ingredients, according to each recipe.

Savarin with Ice Cream and Caramel Sauce

(serves 6)
Preparation time without baking savarin: about 20 min
Unsuitable for the freezer

1 large or 6 small individual savarins
1 portion sugar syrup (see basic recipe)
75ml (3fl oz) rum or brandy
1 litre (1¾pt) vanilla, tutti frutti or chocolate ice cream
250ml (9fl oz) double cream
25g (1oz) flaked almonds
For the caramel sauce:
175g (6oz) sugar
200–250ml (7–9fl oz) water

1 Stir rum or brandy into warm sugar syrup and sprinkle over the cake, as in basic recipe. Whip the cream and toast almond flakes until golden.

2 Put the sugar in a warm, dry frying pan and shake carefully, until sugar starts to melt. Do not stir, or the sugar may become lumpy. When sugar is golden brown, add water and boil, stirring all the time, until smooth. Pour sauce into a jug or bowl and leave to cool.

3 Turn out large savarin onto a serving dish or put small ones on individual plates. Spoon half the ice cream into the savarin(s) and pour caramel sauce on top. Shape the remaining ice cream into balls and place in the centre. Decorate with piped cream and toasted almond flakes.

Savarin with Fruit Salad

(serves 6)
Preparation time without baking savarin: about 20 min
Unsuitable for the freezer

1 savarin
1 portion sugar syrup (see basic recipe)

75ml (3fl oz) orange liqueur or 100ml (4fl oz) orange juice
1 fresh pineapple or 1 can pineapple segments
about 300g (11oz) black grapes
1 jar maraschino cherries
2 pears or peaches

1 Stir orange liqueur or juice into the warm sugar syrup and spoon over the hot cake.

2 Peel and slice pineapple or drain canned pineapple. Rinse grapes, halve and remove pips. Peel and cube pears or peaches. Mix all the fruit and sprinkle with a little syrup from the cherries, and a little more orange liqueur.

3 Fill savarin with some of the fruit salad. Serve the remainder separately. Accompany the savarin with whipped cream.

Strawberry Savarin

(serves 6)
Preparation time, without baking savarin: about 20 min
Unsuitable for the freezer

1 savarin
1 portion sugar syrup (see basic recipe)

100ml (4fl oz) port or 2 × 15ml tbsp (2tbsp) fruit liqueur
500g (1lb 2oz) firm strawberries
maraschino cherries
4 × 15ml tbsp (4tbsp) redcurrant jelly or apricot jam

1 Stir port or fruit liqueur into sugar syrup and spoon half over the warm savarin.

2 Mix redcurrant jelly or sieved apricot jam with 2–3 × 15ml tbsp (2–3tbsp) sugar syrup. Place halved maraschino cherries on savarin and spoon over remaining sugar syrup to make them stay in place.

3 Spread jelly or jam carefully over cake. Instead of using this glaze, you can make an extra portion of sugar syrup and boil it until you can pull it out of saucepan in thin threads with a spoon. If this is poured over cake very slowly and carefully it will set. Fill savarin with strawberries and serve with cream or soured cream.

Below: Savarin with Fruit Salad is served with a bowl of whipped cream.

The Ever-popular Pie

A pie makes a perfect follow-up to a light main course. And because it contains fruit such as lemons, apples and pears it is never too heavy and has a lovely fresh flavour.

Cream Apple Pie (left)
(serves 5–6)
Preparation time: 25–30 min
Baking time: 20–25 min
Oven temperature: 200°C, 400°F, Gas 6
Unsuitable for the freezer

about 750g (1½lb) cooking apples
sugar to taste
5–6 rusks or thick slices white bread slowly dried out in the oven until crisp
100g (4oz) soft light brown sugar
2–3 × 15ml tbsp (2–3tbsp) sweet sherry
25g (1oz) butter
2 eggs
2 egg yolks
a few drops of vanilla essence
250ml (9fl oz) single cream
1 × 15ml tbsp (1tbsp) cornflour
50g (2oz) almonds

1 Peel, core and slice apples. Stew with 50–100ml (2–4fl oz) water and sugar to taste, to a stiff purée. Cool.
2 Crumble rusks or dried bread and sprinkle with brown sugar and sherry. Grease an ovenproof dish thoroughly and fill with alternate layers of crumbled rusks and apple purée.

3 Whisk whole eggs and egg yolks with 3–4 × 15ml tbsp (3–4tbsp) sugar, vanilla essence, cream and cornflour in a heavy-based saucepan. Heat, whisking all the time, until thick and smooth, but do not allow to boil. Blanch the almonds, chop finely and add to custard mixture.
4 Cover apple with custard and bake in the oven until golden. Serve warm with whipped cream or vanilla ice cream.

Lemon Meringue Pie (centre)
(serves 4–6)
Preparation time: 25–30 min
Resting time for pastry: 1 hr
Baking time: about 25 min
Oven temperature (middle shelf): 200°C, 400°F, Gas 6
Unsuitable for the freezer

For the pastry:
125g (4½oz) butter

175g (6oz) plain flour
1–2 × 15ml tbsp (1–2tbsp) caster
  sugar
1 egg yolk
For the filling:
2 eggs
juice of 1 lemon
2 egg yolks
250ml (9fl oz) milk
4 × 15ml tbsp (4tbsp) caster sugar
2 × 15ml tbsp (2tbsp) cornflour
1 × 5ml tsp (5tsp) grated lemon zest
For the meringue:
3 egg whites
100g (4oz) caster sugar

1 Sift flour into a bowl and rub in butter. Add sugar and egg yolk, mixing it in with your finger tips. Quickly knead dough and leave to rest in a cold place for at least 1 hr.
2 Roll out dough and place in a well greased and floured flan tin (preferably a tin with a fluted edge), about 20cm (8in) in diameter. Prick pastry well with a fork, weigh down with foil and baking beans. Bake blind for about 15 min then cool.
3 Whisk together whole eggs, egg yolks, sugar, milk, lemon juice, cornflour and finely grated lemon zest in a heavy-based saucepan, whisking vigorously all the time, until the mixture is smooth. Do not allow to boil. Cool, stirring occasionally.
4 Whisk egg whites until standing in stiff peaks, then whisk in the sugar a little at a time. Spoon lemon mixture into pastry base and cover with meringue. Bake in the oven for a further 10 min. Serve warm.

French Pear Pie (right)
(serves 4–6)
Preparation time: 25–30 min
Resting time for pastry: about 1 hr
Baking time: 25–30 min
Oven temperature (middle shelf):
200°C, 400°F, Gas 6
Unsuitable for the freezer

1 quantity pastry as for Lemon
  Meringue Pie
15g (½oz) butter
6 pears
100ml (4fl oz) double cream
2 × 15ml tbsp (2tbsp) icing sugar
2 × 5ml tsp (2tsp) ground ginger
½–1 × 5ml tsp (½–1tsp) ground
  cinnamon
½ beaten egg

1 Knead pastry lightly and set aside in a cold place for 1 hr. Grease an ovenproof dish. Peel, core and quarter pears and arrange in the prepared dish. Mix together cream, sifted icing sugar and ginger and sprinkle over pears. Finally, sprinkle with a little cinnamon.
2 Roll out pastry and use it to cover pears. Seal carefully around the edges, brush with beaten egg and bake as indicated.
Serve warm with whipped cream or ice-cold soured cream.

Veiled Rhubarb is a tasty everyday dessert made from left-over stewed rhubarb.

Stewed Rhubarb

(serves 4–5)
Preparation time: about 10 min
Cooking time: 15–20 min
Unsuitable for the freezer

750g (1½lb) rhubarb
750ml (1¼pt) water
½ vanilla pod
sugar to taste
3 × 15ml tbsp (3tbsp) arrowroot
artificial colouring, if liked

1 Trim rhubarb and cut into small pieces. Simmer in water until tender with ½ vanilla pod.
2 Remove vanilla pod. Sweeten with sugar to taste. Add artificial colouring, if liked, or colour with blackcurrant juice.
3 Mix the arrowroot into a paste with about 100ml (4fl oz) cold water. Remove saucepan from heat and whisk in paste. Pour rhubarb into a serving dish. Sprinkle with a little sugar to prevent a skin from forming.
Serve rhubarb cold with cream. It can be sprinkled with finely chopped almonds if you wish.

Luxury Rhubarb Dessert

(serves 4–5)
Preparation time: about 10 min
Unsuitable for the freezer

1 quantity rhubarb compote (see right)
8–10 macaroons
2 × 15ml tbsp (2tbsp) port
250ml (9fl oz) double cream
brown sugar to serve

1 Crush macaroons coarsely and sprinkle with port mixed with 1–2 × 15ml tbsp (1–2tbsp) juice from rhubarb compote.
2 Place macaroons and rhubarb in layers in a serving dish and cover with a thick layer of whipped cream. Sprinkle brown sugar over. Serve cold with a glass of port.

Rhubarb Desserts

Veiled Rhubarb

(serves 4)
Preparation time: about 15 min
Unsuitable for the freezer

1 quantity stewed rhubarb (see right)
8–10 rusks or thick slices white bread
   dried out in the oven
4–6 × 15ml tbsp (4–6tbsp) sugar
15g (½oz) butter
100–200ml (4–7fl oz) double cream

1 Crumble rusks or bread coarsely, mix with sugar and sauté in butter in a frying pan. Cool a little and place in layers with the rhubarb in a bowl, reserving some of the dried rusk for decoration.
2 Whip cream and spoon over top. Sprinkle with reserved rusks. Serve warm or cold.

Rhubarb Soup Dessert

(serves 4–5)
Preparation time: about 10 min
Cooking time: about 15 min
Unsuitable for the freezer

500–750g (1lb 2oz–1½lb) rhubarb
1½litres (2½pt) water
1 vanilla pod or cinnamon stick
sugar to taste
2 × 15ml tbsp (2tbsp) arrowroot per
   litre (1¾pt) purée

1 Chop rhubarb and boil in water with vanilla pod or cinnamon stick until tender.
2 Remove pod. Press rhubarb through a sieve and sweeten with sugar to taste. Mix arrowroot with about 100ml (4fl oz) cold water. Whisk in arrowroot paste and heat through until thickened. Serve soup warm or ice cold with crisp, thin sweet biscuits.

Rhubarb Compote
(serves 4–6)
Preparation time: about 10 min
Cooking time: 10–12 min
Unsuitable for the freezer

500g (1lb 2oz) rhubarb
200ml (7fl oz) water
85–125g (3½–4½oz) sugar
½ vanilla pod

1 Trim rhubarb and peel off any tough parts. Cut stalks into 2cm (¾in) lengths.
2 Make a syrup from sugar, water and ½ vanilla pod. Add rhubarb and simmer for 3–4 min. Remove saucepan from heat and leave covered for 8–10 min, or until rhubarb is tender, but not mushy.
3 Remove the rhubarb with a slotted spoon and place in a bowl. Boil up sugar syrup until thick. Pour over rhubarb and set aside to cool.

Luxury Rhubarb Dessert – layer upon layer of rhubarb and crushed macaroons, covered with a thick layer of whipped cream and sprinkled with brown sugar.

Rhubarb Meringue (above)
(serves 4–6)
Preparation time: about 20 min
Cooking time: about 20 min
Oven temperature (middle shelf):
200°C, 400°F, Gas 6
Unsuitable for the freezer

25g (1oz) butter
8 × 15ml tbsp (8tbsp) caster sugar
about 50g (2oz) breadcrumbs
about 400ml (¾pt) rhubarb compote
  (see above)
3 egg whites

1 Melt butter and mix with 4 × 15ml tbsp (4tbsp) sugar and breadcrumbs. Place mixture in an ovenproof dish. Spoon over rhubarb compote (it should not be runny).
2 Whisk egg whites until standing in stiff peaks then whisk in remaining sugar, a little at a time. Spoon over rhubarb and bake as indicated.

Bananas at their Best

Banana Fritters (left)
(serves 4–6)
Preparation time: about 20 min
Resting time for batter: about 30 min
Cooking time: a few min
Unsuitable for the freezer

8–10 small, firm bananas
oil or lard for frying
sugar
1–2 lemons
For the batter:
125g (4½oz) plain flour
½ × 5ml tsp (½tsp) salt
1 egg
100ml (4fl oz) beer
about 100ml (4fl oz) water
25g (1oz) butter

1 Mix flour and salt. Make a well in the centre and add egg yolk, beer, half the water and the melted butter. Whisk to a smooth paste then leave to rest. Stir in more water if batter is too thick – it should have the consistency of pancake batter. Whisk egg white until standing in stiff peaks and fold into batter.
2 Heat oil or lard in a deep frying pan. Peel bananas and cut in half crossways. Dip into batter one by one and lower into fat 3 or 4 at a time. Turn with a slotted spoon until golden brown and crisp on all sides. Drain bananas on absorbent paper as soon as they are cooked. Serve banana fritters warm, sprinkled with sugar to taste and with lemon juice or lemon wedges.

Banana Fritters
1 Mix batter ingredients.

Butterfried Bananas (right)
(serves 4)
Preparation time: about 10 min
Frying time: a few min
Unsuitable for the freezer

4 firm bananas
2–3 × 15ml tbsp (2–3tbsp) clear
  honey
25g (1oz) almonds
25g (1oz) butter
1 lemon
a few raisins (optional)

1 Peel bananas and brush all over
with honey.
2 Flake or coarsely chop almonds.
Turn bananas in almonds and fry
in butter until golden, turning
frequently.
3 Sprinkle generously with lemon
juice. Decorate with thin strips of
lemon zest and raisins, if liked.
Serve with whipped cream.

Flambéed Bananas
(serves 6)
Preparation time: about 15 min
Cooking time: a few min
Unsuitable for the freezer

6 small, firm bananas
25g (1oz) butter
2 × 15ml tbsp (2tbsp) sugar
1 lemon
6 × 15ml tbsp (6tbsp) brandy
  or rum

1 Peel bananas and fry carefully on
all sides in butter. Sprinkle with
sugar and 1 × 15ml tbsp (1tbsp)
finely grated lemon zest and lemon
juice. Heat brandy or rum in a small
covered saucepan.

*2 Cut bananas in two and coat in
batter, one at a time.*

*3 Cook banana halves in oil 3–4 at a
time, until golden brown.*

2 If the bananas are to be flambéed
at the table, place them in a decora-
tive frying pan over a spirit flame.
Pour in heated brandy, shake carefully and tilt pan slightly so that the
spirit flame sets the brandy alight.
Shake pan carefully until flames are
extinguished. (Have a lid handy in
case the brandy burns for too long or
too vigorously.)
Serve with soured or whipped
cream.
NOTE Many people prefer to flambée
the bananas at the table, but this
operation can also be carried out in
the kitchen. Set the brandy or rum
alight with a match. Otherwise, pro-
ceed as described above.

Decorative Fruit Salads

Spanish Orange Salad (left)
(serves 4–5)
Preparation time: about 15 min
Unsuitable for the freezer

4–5 sweet oranges
2 bananas
150ml (¼pt) sweet sherry
25–50g (1–2oz) cooking chocolate

1 Peel oranges and remove all the pith. Put on a plate and slice. Peel and chop bananas and turn immediately in orange juice on plate.
2 Mix fruit in a serving bowl and pour the sweet sherry over. Grate cooking chocolate over dessert and decorate with curls of orange peel. Serve with a glass of sweet sherry.

Stuffed Oranges (see cover)
A simple and easy fruit dessert with oranges and soured cream. For 6 oranges allow: 100ml (4fl oz) soured cream, 2–3 × 15ml tbsp (2–3tbsp) sugar, about 50g (2oz) walnuts and 2 × 15ml tbsp (2tbsp) liqueur of your choice. Cut the tops off the oranges, scoop out the flesh and cut into neat pieces. Mix with soured cream, sugar, liqueur and a few coarsely chopped nuts.
Fill the orange shells with this mixture and decorate with walnut halves.

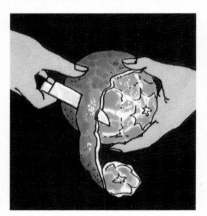

To Segment an Orange
1 Peel orange. Remove as much of the pith as possible.

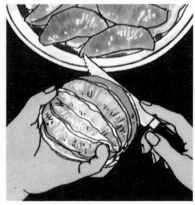

2 Using a sharp knife, remove each segment, cutting just inside the membrane on both sides.

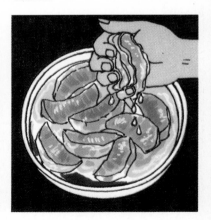

3 Place orange segments in a bowl and squeeze out any juice left in membranes over them.

Melon Salad (below)
(serves 4)
Preparation time: about 15 min
Chilling time: about 1 hr
Unsuitable for the freezer

½ honeydew melon weighing
    400–500g (about 1lb)
2 bananas
1 can mandarin orange segments
100–150ml (4–5fl oz) sweet white
    wine
3 × 15ml tbsp (3tbsp) orange juice
1 small bunch of green grapes

1 Peel and deseed the melon and slice flesh neatly. Place in a dish and refrigerate for 1 hr.
2 Mix orange juice and white wine in a bowl and add some of the syrup from the oranges. Peel bananas and slice directly into mixture.
3 Rinse grapes, halve and remove all pips. Mix with banana slices, well drained mandarin orange segments and melon pieces. Spoon into individual glasses. Serve immediately with cream.

Fruit Salad with Port Flavoured Cream

(serves 4–5)
Preparation time: about 30 min
Unsuitable for the freezer

2 oranges
3 pears
2 apples
2 bananas
4 kiwi fruit
1 bunch black grapes
4 fresh or 1 can peaches
1 lemon
25–50g (1–2oz) almonds
For the port flavoured cream :
1 egg
2 egg yolks
4 × 15ml tbsp (4tbsp) sugar
100ml (4fl oz) tawny port
250ml (9fl oz) double cream

1 Peel oranges and remove all pith. On a plate, slice oranges thinly. Cut slices into 4 and transfer juice to a bowl.
2 Peel apples, pears and bananas and slice thinly straight into orange juice. Pour juice of ½ lemon over and mix well to prevent discoloration.
3 Dip fresh peaches into boiling water for a moment or two. Rinse in cold water and peel. Halve peaches, remove stones and dice. Mix immediately with apples and pears. Place orange pieces on top. Peel and slice kiwi fruit. Rinse grapes, halve and remove all pips. Blanch and flake almonds.
4 Whisk the whole egg, egg yolks and sugar until standing in soft peaks. Whisk in port and place bowl over a saucepan of boiling water. Whisk vigorously until thick and fluffy. Remove bowl from saucepan and leave to cool, whisking frequently. Whip cream and mix into port flavoured mixture.
5 Mix fruit carefully with almond flakes and spoon into individual glasses or a large serving bowl. Spoon a large portion of port flavoured cream over each portion and serve the rest separately.

Cream for Fruit Salads

(serves 4)
Preparation time: about 10 min
Unsuitable for the freezer

2 egg yolks
3 × 15ml tbsp (3tbsp) icing sugar
250ml (9fl oz) double cream
2 × 15ml tbsp (2tbsp) brandy, rum,
    sherry, liqueur, white wine or
    orange juice

1 Whisk egg yolks with icing sugar until stiff. Mix in brandy, rum, wine or fruit juice to taste and to complement the flavour of the fruit salad.
2 Whip cream and fold in the whisked egg yolks with a rubber spatula. Serve immediately.

Four Fresh Berry Favourites

Raspberries with Orange Cream

(serves 4)
Preparation time: 15–20 min
Unsuitable for the freezer

about 500g (1lb 2oz) fresh or frozen
    raspberries
3 egg yolks
2 × 15ml tbsp (2tbsp) sugar
1 orange
½ lemon
1 × 15ml tbsp (1tbsp) orange liqueur
250ml (9fl oz) double cream
raspberry liqueur (optional)

1 Rinse raspberries if necessary and clean, or defrost frozen berries. Marinate in raspberry liqueur if liked. Sprinkle frozen, defrosted raspberries with a little sugar.

2 Thoroughly mix egg yolks with sugar, lemon juice, finely grated orange and lemon zest. Whip cream and stir in egg yolks and orange liqueur.

3 Spoon raspberries into individual glasses and pour cream over. Decorate with orange or lemon twists. Serve immediately.

Berries in Syrup with Ice Cream

(serves 4)
Preparation time: about 15 min
Marinating time: about 1 hr
Unsuitable for the freezer

about 500g (1lb 2oz) mixed berries
    (redcurrants, blackcurrants,
    raspberries, bilberries or other)
500ml (1pt) vanilla ice cream
about 200ml (7fl oz) double cream
    or Cream Ice (see page 56)
25g (1oz) almonds
For the syrup:
100ml (4fl oz) water
85g (3½oz) sugar
200ml (7fl oz) white wine

1 Rinse berries and drain well. Make a syrup of sugar and water, cool, then stir in wine. Pour over berries, cover and place in the refrigerator.

2 Whip cream. Blanch and flake almonds. Sauté almond flakes until golden in a dry frying pan.

3 Spoon berries and syrup into chilled individual glasses or dishes. Place a scoop of vanilla ice cream on top and decorate with lightly whipped cream and almond flakes.
Serve immediately.

VARIATION:
Sugar syrup can be made with a fruit wine (blackcurrant or elderberry wine) instead of white wine.

Strawberry Mousse

(serves 4)
Preparation time: 15–20 min
Unsuitable for the freezer

about 250g (9oz) fresh or frozen
  strawberries
3–4 × 15ml tbsp (3–4tbsp) sugar
2 egg whites
250ml (9fl oz) double cream

1 Rinse berries if necessary. Hull them or defrost frozen berries. Set aside 4 large, perfect fruits and work the rest in a blender with the sugar. Alternatively, mash the berries to a pulp with a fork and whisk them with sugar.
2 Whisk egg whites until standing in stiff peaks and whip cream lightly. Reserve some of the cream for decoration.
3 Carefully fold whisked egg whites and cream into strawberry purée and spoon into chilled individual glasses. Decorate with cream and whole strawberries. Serve at once.

TIP
If you want to make the mousse in advance, mix 8g (¼oz) dissolved gelatine into the strawberry purée to prevent the mousse collapsing.

Strawberries in Almond Cream

(serves 4)
Preparation time: about 20 min
Chilling time: 1–2 hr
Unsuitable for the freezer

300–400g (11–14oz) strawberries
4 egg yolks
4 × 15ml tbsp (4tbsp) sugar
a few drops of vanilla essence
50g (2oz) almonds
250ml (9fl oz) single cream

1 Rinse berries if necessary, hull them and sprinkle with a little sugar. Whisk egg yolks, sugar and vanilla essence until standing in soft peaks.
2 Blanch almonds and allow to dry. Grind almonds or chop them finely. Put almonds into a saucepan, pour in cream and bring to the boil.
3 Pour boiling almond cream into whisked egg mixture, whisking vigorously all the time. Return to saucepan and whisk over low heat until cream thickens, but do not allow to boil.
4 Cool almond cream, stirring frequently, cover and refrigerate for about 1 hr.
Place strawberries and cream in layers in individual glasses. Serve at once.

Left to right: Raspberries with Orange Cream; Berries in Syrup with Ice Cream; Strawberry Mousse; Strawberries in Almond Cream.

Apples – Economical and Tasty

Caramelized Apples (below)
(serves 6)
Preparation time: about 30 min
Baking time: 10–20 min depending on type of apples used
Oven temperature (middle shelf): 200°C, 400°F, Gas 6
Unsuitable for the freezer

6 large, firm apples
65g (2½oz) butter
350g (12oz) sugar
25–50g (1–2oz) almonds

1 Grease an ovenproof dish with 25g (1oz) butter. Peel and core the apples, and brush with 25g (1oz) melted butter. Roll apples in about 100g (4oz) sugar and place in dish.
2 Bake apples in the oven. The exact time depends on the variety of the apples, their size, the time of year and how they have been stored. Do not bake them for too long or they will collapse.
3 Blanch and flake almonds. Melt the remaining sugar in a frying pan without stirring. When sugar is lightly browned, remove pan from heat. Immediately stir in remaining butter.
4 Take apples out of oven. Fill with almonds and pour caramel over. (If you do not want the sauce to set, bring it to the boil with 100ml (4fl oz) water before pouring over.
Serve apples warm with Vanilla Cream (see page 17) or ice cream.

Apple Trifles
(serves 6)
Preparation time: about 15 min
Unsuitable for the freezer

6 large macaroons
2–3 × 15ml tbsp (2–3tbsp) sherry or madeira
300–400ml (½–¾pt) firm apple purée
250ml (9fl oz) double cream
25–50g (1–2oz) almonds

1 Place one macaroon on each of 6 individual plates and sprinkle with sweet or medium fortified wine. Blanch almonds and flake or chop coarsely.
2 Cover macaroons with apple purée and lightly whipped cream. Decorate with almonds and serve at once.

VARIATION:
Instead of whipped cream you can make the trifle with Vanilla Cream (see page 17) or boiled cream. To make the latter, take 1 egg, 1 egg yolk, 2 × 15ml tbsp (2tbsp) sugar, 1 × 15ml tbsp (1tbsp) cornflour and 250ml (9fl oz) milk or half cream. Stir together in a saucepan and whisk over low heat until the mixture is thick and smooth. During cooling, whip from time to time. Whip 100ml (4fl oz) double cream until stiff and mix with the boiled cream.

Apples with Jam
(serves 4–5)
Preparation time: about 20 min
Baking time: 10–20 min depending on type of apples used
Oven temperature (middle shelf): 200°C, 400°F, Gas 6
Unsuitale for the freezer

5 large, firm apples
25g (1oz) butter
lemon juice
50g (2oz) icing sugar
200–300ml (7–10fl oz) apple juice
100–200ml (4–7fl oz) double cream
blackcurrant or bilberry jam

1 Peel and core apples. Fill with a mixture of softened butter and icing sugar and brush with lemon juice.
2 Grease an ovenproof dish and place apples in it. Pour in apple juice and bake until apples are tender.
3 Remove dish from oven. Pour cream into dish and fill apples with jam.

Apples with Jam is a delicious dessert – both as family and party fare.

Other fillings for baked apples:

Marzipan Filling
Mix together 50–75g (2–3oz) ground almonds with 2 × 15ml tbsp (2tbsp) icing sugar and 1 lightly beaten egg. Fill apples with the mixture and bake as indicated. Sprinkle with sifted icing sugar before serving.

Raisin Filling
Mix 25g (1oz) softened butter with 1 × 15 tbsp (1tbsp) sugar, 1 × 15 tbsp (1tbsp) port and 100g (4oz) raisins. Fill apples and bake them.

Cinnamon Filling
Mix 25g (1oz) softened butter with 2 × 15ml tbsp (2tbsp) sugar and 2 × 5ml tsp (2tsp) ground cinnamon. Fill and bake apples. Sprinkle with a mixture of sugar and cinnamon before serving.

Macaroon Filling
Fill apples with crushed macaroons and sprinkle with 25g (1oz) melted butter. Bake apples and sprinkle with chopped almonds before serving.

Orange Filling
Mix together 2 × 15ml tbsp (2tbsp) firm orange marmalade, 2 × 15ml tbsp (2tbsp) orange juice and 1 × 5ml tsp (1tsp) grated orange peel. Fill apples and bake with a little orange juice in dish.

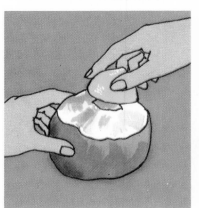

Baked Apples
1 Remove core with a knife.

2 Squeeze lemon over apples to prevent discoloration.

3 Fill apples, place in an ovenproof dish and bake as in recipe.

Meringued Apples (left)

(serves 4)
Preparation time: about 20 min
Baking time: 10–20 min in all, depending on type of apples used
Oven temperature (middle shelf): 200 °C, 400 °F, Gas 6
Unsuitable for the freezer

4 large, firm apples
2 × 15ml tbsp (2tbsp) sugar
1 × 5ml tsp (1tsp) ground cinnamon
25g (1oz) butter
For the meringue :
2 egg whites
100g (4oz) caster sugar
8–10 almonds

1 Wipe and core apples and peel top half. Sprinkle sugar and cinnamon over apples and place in well greased ovenproof dish. Place a knob of butter on each apple and bake until barely tender.
2 Whisk egg whites until standing in stiff peaks then whisk in the sugar, 1 × 15ml tbsp (1tbsp) at a time. Spoon meringue mixture into a piping bag. Finely chop almonds.
3 Remove dish from oven. Pipe a rosette of meringue mixture on each apple and sprinkle with chopped almonds. Bake for 6–8 min or until meringue is golden. Serve apples warm with a cold or warm dessert sauce made from cherry, raspberry or strawberry juice thickened with a little cornflour worked to a paste with cold water.

Cranberry Apples (left)

(serves 4)
Preparation time: about 20 min
Baking time: 10–20 min depending on type of apples used
Oven temperature (middle shelf): 200 °C, 400 °F, Gas 6
Unsuitable for the freezer

4–6 large, firm apples
juice of ½ lemon
15g (½oz) butter
about 8 × 15ml tbsp (8tbsp)
  cranberry sauce
1 pear
1 × 15ml tbsp (1tbsp) rum
  (optional)
2 egg whites
4 × 15ml tbsp (4tbsp) sugar

1 Wipe apples, cut off tops and remove cores. Sprinkle with lemon juice and place in a well greased

ovenproof dish.

2 Fill apples with a mixture of cranberry sauce and peeled, chopped pear and flavour with rum if liked. Bake apples until barely tender.

3 Whisk egg whites until standing in stiff peaks and whisk in sugar, a little at a time. Remove dish from oven and place a spoonful of meringue mixture on each apple. Bake for 6–8 min or until meringue is golden. Serve warm.

Delicious Apple Compote (right)

(serves 4)
Preparation time: about 20 min
Cooking time: about 15 min in all
Unsuitable for the freezer

4 large pippin or firm dessert apples
For the cooking syrup:
100ml (4fl oz) water
85g (3½oz) sugar
1 whole clove
½ lemon
1 small cinnamon stick
200–300ml (7–10fl oz) sweet white wine

1 Make a syrup of sugar, water, lemon juice and grated zest of ½ lemon, clove and cinnamon. Boil for about 10 min then remove saucepan from heat. Stir in white wine.

2 Peel and core apples, then cut thin slices straight into syrup.
Simmer apples over low heat until barely tender. Do not allow apple slices to disintegrate. Cool apples in syrup then remove clove and cinnamon. Serve cold with cream.

Veiled Lady

(serves 4–6)
Preparation time: 20–30 min
Unsuitable for the freezer

about 750g (1½lb) good quality apples
sugar to taste
150–200g (5–7oz) crushed rusk or dried white bread
2–3 × 15ml tbsp (2–3tbsp) sugar
25–40g (1–1½oz) butter
about 6 × 15ml tbsp (6tbsp) strawberry jam
250ml (9fl oz) double cream

1 Make a firm apple purée by cooking peeled, sliced apples in water. Sweeten with sugar and cool.

2 Mix crushed rusk or dried bread with sugar and fry in butter in a frying pan, stirring all the time to avoid burning. Cool, stirring often, to prevent lumps forming.

3 Layer rusk mixture, jam and apple purée in a dish or bowl, ending with a layer of rusk. Whip cream stiffly and pipe over dessert.

Old-fashioned Apple Dessert

(serves 6)
Preparation time: about 20 min
Unsuitable for the freezer

about 1kg (2lb) juicy apples
85g (3½oz) sugar
100g (4oz) breadcrumbs
25–40g (1–1½oz) butter
50g (2oz) almonds
250ml (9fl oz) double cream
redcurrant or apple jelly

1 Peel and core apples. Slice and stew in a little water until barely tender. (Very juicy apples can be cooked, covered, without water.) Sweeten with 2–3 × 15ml tbsp (2–3tbsp) sugar and cool.

2 Mix breadcrumbs, remaining sugar and blanched chopped almonds and fry in butter in frying pan, stirring all the time to prevent burning and sticking.

3 Layer apples, breadcrumb mixture and lightly whipped cream in a dish, ending with a layer of cream. Decorate with redcurrant or apple jelly and serve immediately.

The apples can be boiled and breadcrumbs fried well in advance, but the dessert should not be assembled until just before serving time.

French Apple Pie

(serves 6)
Preparation time: about 30 min
Resting time for dough: about 1 hr
Baking time: 30–40 min
Oven temperature (middle shelf):
200°C, 400°F, Gas 6
Unsuitable for the freezer

For the pastry :
100g (4oz) butter
150g (5oz) flour
2 × 15ml tbsp (2tbsp) caster sugar
1 egg
For the filling :
750g (1½lb) juicy apples
85g (3½oz) sugar
1 × 5ml tsp (1tsp) ground cinnamon
100g (4oz) raisins
25g (1oz) butter
100ml (4fl oz) double cream

1 Rub butter into flour until the mixture resembles fine breadcrumbs. Add sugar and ½ beaten egg and quickly form into a dough. Leave in a cool place to rest for about 1 hr.
2 Peel, core and slice apples and place in a greased ovenproof dish. Sprinkle with sugar and cinnamon then sprinkle with raisins and dot with butter.
3 Roll out the pastry so that it is a little larger than dish. Place over apples and trim the edges. Make a hole in the middle of lid. Make a funnel from a piece of foil and press into hole. Roll out thin pieces of remaining pastry into a thin sausage shape and place round pastry edge and around funnel. Brush with beaten egg and bake as indicated.
4 Just before the pie is cooked pour in the cream through the funnel, then remove foil.
Serve hot or warm.

Apple Crumble

(serves 6)
Preparation time: about 15 min
Baking time: about 40 min
Oven temperature (middle shelf):
200°C, 400°F, Gas 6
Unsuitable for the freezer

about 750g (1½lb) juicy apples
juice of 1 lemon
100g (4oz) sultanas
4 × 15ml tbsp (4tbsp) sugar
1 × 5ml tsp (1tsp) ground cinnamon
For the crumble :
125 g (4½oz) butter
125g (4½oz) plain flour
85g (3½oz) sugar
50g (2oz) almonds

1 Peel, core and quarter apples, slice thinly into half moons. Arrange in a well greased ovenproof dish. Squeeze lemon juice over immediately and mix apples with sultanas, sugar and cinnamon.
2 Rub butter into flour until it resembles fine breadcrumbs. Add sugar and coarsely chopped almonds and mix well. Sprinkle evenly over apples. Bake as indicated.
Serve hot or warm with lightly whipped cream or soft vanilla ice cream.

Almond Apple Cake

(serves 4–6)
Preparation time: about 15 min
Baking time: about 45 min
Oven temperature (middle shelf):
200°C, 400°F, Gas 6

about 1kg (2lb) firm, good quality apples
juice of 1 lemon
100–200ml (4–7fl oz) white wine or apple juice
175g (6oz) sugar
a few drops of vanilla essence
100g (4oz) breadcrumbs
100g (4oz) butter
50g (2oz) almonds

1 Grease an ovenproof dish with 25g (1oz) butter. Peel and core apples and slice into dish. Squeeze lemon juice over at once. Pour wine or apple juice into dish and cover with foil. Bake for 10 min.
2 Mix sugar, vanilla essence and breadcrumbs and sprinkle over apples. Melt remaining butter and sprinkle over the top then return to the oven and bake, uncovered, for a further 30–35 min. Sprinkle with blanched, flaked almonds for the last 5 min of baking time. Serve warm with whipped cream.

French Apple Pie is deliciously and delicately spiced.

New Ways with Fruit

Fruit desserts need not be boring, surprise your family and friends with pears in port served with almond brittle, figs flambéed at the table or peaches accompanied by raspberry purée and ice cream.

Flambéed Figs (below)
(serves 4–6)
Preparation time: about 20 min
Unsuitable for the freezer

*1 large can of figs weighing about
    450g (1lb)
25–50g (1–2oz) almonds
40g (1½oz) butter
juice of 1 lemon
85g (3½oz) sugar
50ml (2fl oz) Pernod or brandy*

1 Put figs into a sieve placed over a bowl and drain well. Reserve the juice. Blanch and flake almonds. Sautée until golden in 15g (½oz) butter.
2 Remove almonds. Add sugar and the remaining butter to pan and cook over low to moderate heat until lightly golden. Add about 200ml (7fl oz) fig juice and lemon juice and boil, stirring, until sauce is smooth.
3 Place figs in an oven-to-table sauté pan and pour sauce over. Carefully heat on hot plate or over spirit flame at the table. Pour in heated Pernod or brandy, shake pan carefully and set alight with a match. Shake pan carefully until flames die down. Always keep a lid handy when flambéeing and quickly place it over the pan if flames burn too long or too fiercely. Serve at once.

Pears with Almond Meringue
(serves 4–6)
Preparation time: about 30 min
Springform tin about 20cm (8in) in diameter
Baking time: about 30 min
Oven temperature (middle shelf):
150–160°C, 300–325°F, Gas 2–3
Unsuitable for the freezer

*For the Almond Meringue:
75–100g (3–4oz) almonds
85g (3½oz) caster sugar
50g (2oz) breadcrumbs
¾ × 5ml tsp (¾tsp) baking powder
3 large egg whites
For the filling:
6 large pears
85g (3½oz) caster sugar
150ml (¼pt) sweet white wine
½ vanilla pod
1 jar maraschino cherries
200ml (7fl oz) double cream or
    soured cream
2 × 15ml tbsp (2tbsp) port or
    madeira
For the chocolate sauce:
150g (5oz) cooking chocolate
15g (½oz) butter
4 × 15ml tbsp (4tbsp) double cream*

1 Blanch almonds for the almond meringue, dry and grind in a nut mill, blender or food processor. Add sugar, breadcrumbs and baking powder and fold in stiffly beaten egg whites. Grease and flour a springform tin and spoon in mixture. Bake as indicated and leave to cool.
2 Make a syrup of sugar, 300ml (½pt) water and ½ vanilla pod. Add white wine and peeled, halved pears. Poach pears until barely tender and leave to cool in syrup.
3 Break chocolate into small pieces and melt in a heavy-based saucepan with butter and cream over low heat, stirring until smooth. Keep warm.
4 About 1 hr before serving, sprinkle almond meringue with port

or madeira and cover completely with lightly whipped cream or soured cream. Place well drained pears and maraschino cherries on top and pour some of the chocolate sauce over. Serve the remaining sauce separately.

Pears in Port
(serves 4)
Preparation time: about 20 min
Cooking time: 10–20 min depending on type of pears used
Unsuitable for the freezer

8 small, firm pears
For the syrup:
1 orange
200–300ml (7–10fl oz) port
150g (5oz) sugar
For the almond brittle:
85g (3½oz) sugar
a large pinch of baking powder
For the Crème Chantilly:
250ml (9fl oz) double cream
1–2 × 15ml tbsp (1–2tbsp) icing sugar
a few drops of vanilla essence

1 Melt sugar for almond brittle in dry frying pan. Shake pan carefully, but do not stir until it is golden and liquid. Stir in baking powder to make almond brittle porous and pour in a thin layer onto a sheet of greaseproof paper brushed with oil.
2 Scrub orange in hot water with a stiff brush, rinse in cold water and dry. Peel orange thinly with a potato peeler (only the orange part of the peel should be removed) and place in a sieve. Pour over boiling water then chop peel or cut into thin strips.
3 Make a syrup of port, sugar, orange juice and peel. Peel pears, scrape stems (which should be left on) and poach until barely tender in port syrup. Place pears and syrup in a dish and cool. Sprinkle with crushed almond brittle. Serve pears with Crème Chantilly: whip cream until stiff and flavour with icing sugar and vanilla.

Above right: Pears in Port are sprinkled with almond brittle and served with lightly whipped cream.
Right: Pears with Almond Meringue looks impressive but in fact is simple to make.

Dried fruit in profusion. Here, Fruit Compote is served with lightly whipped cream.

Fruit Fool
(serves 4–6)
Preparation time: about 10 min plus overnight soaking
Cooking time: about 20 min
Unsuitable for the freezer

350–400g (12–14oz) dried fruit
about 1 litre (1¾pt) water
sugar to taste
2–3 × 15ml tbsp (2–3tbsp)
  arrowroot

1 Soak fruit in cold water overnight. Boil until tender in soaking water. Cool a little then press through a sieve or work in a blender, including all the liquid.
2 Bring fruit purée to the boil, remove from the heat. Sweeten with sugar to taste then stir in a paste of arrowroot mixed with a little water. Pour into a serving dish and sprinkle surface with sugar to prevent a skin forming. Serve cold with cream.

Fruit Compote
(serves 4–6)
Preparation time: about 15 min plus overnight soaking
Cooking time: 10–15 min
Cooling time: about 2 hr
Unsuitable for the freezer

about 200g (7oz) dried apricots
about 200g (7oz) dried figs
about 150g (5oz) prunes
about 100g (4oz) raisins
sugar to taste
juice of 1 lemon

Dried Fruit

Dried fruit such as prunes, apricots, figs and raisins are wonderful store-cupboard standbys and can be used to make some easy traditional and unusual desserts.

1 Barely cover all fruit xcept raisins with water, cover and leave in cool place overnight.
2 Boil fruit until barely tender, add raisins and remove saucepan from heat. Set aside for about 20 min, then add lemon juice and sweeten to taste with sugar.
3 Remove fruit with a slotted spoon and place in a dish. Boil up the syrup for a while and pour over fruit. Set aside to cool. Serve cold with lightly whipped cream.

Fruit Soup Dessert

(serves 4–5)
Preparation time: about 10 min plus overnight soaking
Cooking time: 15–25 min
Unsuitable for the freezer

about 200g (7oz) dried fruit
about 1½ litres (2½pt) water
sugar to taste
about 2 × 15ml tbsp (2tbsp)
  arrowroot

1 Select one or several kinds of dried fruit according to taste and soak overnight in cold water.
2 Boil fruit until tender in soaking water and add sugar to taste. Add arrowroot mixed with a little cold water to thicken.
Serve hot or cold with thin, crisp biscuits, macaroons or croûtons sprinkled with sugar.

VARIATION
The fruit can be finely chopped before boiling, or sieved or blended after boiling.

Prune Ring

(serves 6)
Preparation time: about 20 min plus overnight soaking
Cooking time: 15–20 min
Cooling time: 2–3 hr
Unsuitable for the freezer

about 250g (9oz) stoned prunes
500ml (1pt) water
sugar
20g (¾oz) gelatine
200ml (7fl oz) port
1–2 × 15ml tbsp (1–2tbsp) lemon
  juice
250ml (9fl oz) double cream
12 small macaroons

1 Soak prunes in water overnight. Sprinkle gelatine over 4 × 15ml tbsp (4tbsp) cold water and leave to soak for 5 min. Simmer prunes until tender in soaking water with sugar to taste. Remove with slotted spoon. Dissolve gelatine over a saucepan of boiling water. Add port, lemon juice and prune juice.
2 Pour some of the prune jelly into a ring mould of about 1 litre (1¾pt) capacity and allow to set. Arrange prunes in mould (large ones can be sliced), pour over more jelly and allow to set. Fill mould completely with jelly, cover with foil and set

aside in a cold place.
3 When jelly is completely set, loosen around the edges with a knife. Dip mould into very hot water for a few moments, place serving plate over mould, turn over and shake carefully until jelly is unmoulded.
4 Fill prune ring with lightly whipped cream either plain or mixed with crushed macaroons. Arrange macaroons around edge of plate.
Serve well chilled.

Apricot Tart

(serves 6)
Preparation time: about 30 min plus overnight soaking
Cooking time: 20–25 min
Oven temperature (middle shelf): 200°C, 400°F, Gas 6
Unsuitable for the freezer

150–200g (5–7oz) dried apricots
500ml (1pt) water
sugar
1 × 15ml tbsp (1tbsp) cornflour
50g (2oz) almonds
250ml (9fl oz) double cream
375g (12oz) packet frozen puff
  pastry
1 egg
demerara sugar

1 Soak apricots in cold water overnight. Chop fruit into small pieces and boil until tender in soaking water with sugar added to taste. Thicken with cornflour mixed to a

paste with cold water. Defrost pastry.
2 Blanch and halve or coarsely chop almonds. Stir into apricot mixture and cool.
3 Roll out pastry fairly thinly and cut out a circle using a large dinner plate as a guide. Place on baking parchment on a baking sheet, prick with a fork and brush with beaten egg. Using the remaining pastry, cut a thin ring large enough to encircle the base and cut thin strips to form a lattice. Attach 'lattice to ring and place on baking sheet alongside pastry base.
4 Brush all pastry surfaces with beaten egg and sprinkle with demerara sugar. Bake as indicated until base and lattice are nicely golden. Cool for a while on the baking sheet before placing on a wire rack.
5 Just before serving assemble the tart. Whip cream until standing in stiff peaks and spread a thin layer over the pastry base. Spoon in apricot filling and cover with cream. Finally put pastry lattice on top. Serve immediately.

Milk Puddings and Desserts

All over the world, milk is the main ingredient of popular and traditional desserts. The nutritious dishes described here use not just milk but cream, buttermilk and yoghurt too.

Frozen Yoghurt Whip
(serves 4–6)
Preparation time: about 15 min
Freezing time: 2–3 hr

*about 250g (9oz) fresh or frozen
    strawberries or raspberries
sugar to taste
300ml (½pt) natural yoghurt
3 egg whites
250ml (9fl oz) double cream*

1 Rinse fruit if necessary. Hull fresh berries or defrost frozen ones. Purée in a blender with 2–3 × 15ml tbsp (2–3tbsp) sugar.
2 Mix purée with yoghurt, whisk well and sweeten with more sugar if necessary. Transfer mixture to the deep freeze for about 1 hr, stirring from time to time. Remove from the freezer when half frozen.
3 Whisk egg whites until standing in stiff peaks and fold into mixture with 100ml (4fl oz) lightly whipped cream. Return to freezer and leave for about 1–2 hr, stirring several times. Transfer to the refrigerator about 20 min before serving. Stir or whisk mixture and spoon into individual glasses. Decorate with rosettes of whipped cream. Serve immediately.

Buttermilk Mousse
(serves 4–5)
Preparation time: about 10 min
Setting time: 1–2 hr
Suitable for the freezer

15g (½oz) gelatine

*500ml (1pt) buttermilk
3–4 × 15ml tbsp (3–4tbsp) sugar
a few drops of vanilla essence or
    1 × 5ml tsp (1tsp) lemon zest
250ml (9fl oz) double cream*

1 Sprinkle gelatine over 3 × 15ml tbsp (3tbsp) cold water. Sweeten buttermilk with sugar to taste and add vanilla essence or grated lemon zest.
2 Dissolve gelatine over a saucepan of boiling water and pour into buttermilk mixture, stirring vigorously.
3 Whip cream and fold into butter milk mixture. Pour into a serving dish or a ring mould rinsed out with cold water. Leave in a cool place until set then turn out, if desired, and decorate with soft fruit sprinkled with sugar, tinned fruit, warm soft-fruit sauce or other accompaniment.

VARIATION
The mousse can also be made from skimmed milk or natural yoghurt.

Vanilla Dessert
(serves 4–6)
Preparation time: 20 min
Setting time: 1–2 hr
Suitable for the freezer

*15g (½oz) gelatine
4 egg yolks
4 × 15ml tbsp (4tbsp) caster sugar
400ml (¾pt) milk or single cream
1 vanilla pod*

1 Sprinkle gelatine over 3 × 15ml tbsp (3tbsp) cold water then dissolve over hot water. Split vanilla pod open and add to milk or cream and bring to the boil.
2 Whisk egg yolks well with sugar, pour in some of the boiling milk and whisk vigorously. Pour egg and milk mixture back into the pan and heat, stirring, until thick, but do not allow to boil.
3 Remove vanilla pod and add dissolved gelatine, stirring constantly. Pour cream into a jelly mould, rinsed out with cold water. Cover with foil and leave in a cool place to set.
4 Loosen set dessert by running a knife around the edge. Turn out onto a serving dish. Decorate with almond flakes, chopped walnuts, crushed macaroons, grated chocolate or rosettes of cream. Serve cold

with a cold or warm sauce made from fruit juice (see below).

Rum Dessert
Follow the recipe for Vanilla Dessert, but instead of using vanilla, add 50–100ml (2–4fl oz) white rum with the dissolved gelatine. Decorate with whipped cream and grated chocolate.

Fruit Sauce
Heat the contents of a 500g (1lb 2oz) can of cherries with a little water added, until nearly boiling. Thicken sauce with ½–1 × 15ml tbsp (½–1tbsp) cornflour mixed with a little water.
You can also make the sauce from strawberries, raspberries, blackcurrants, redcurrants and other canned fruit. Or you can simply use a fruit juice of your choice.

Chocolate Blancmange
(serves 4)
Preparation time: about 15 min
Unsuitable for the freezer

*800ml (1½pt) milk
3 × 15ml tbsp (3tbsp) arrowroot
2½ × 15ml tbsp (2½tbsp) cocoa
3–4 × 15ml tbsp (3–4tbsp) sugar
a few drops of vanilla essence*

1 Mix together milk, arrowroot, cocoa and sugar in a saucepan and bring to the boil, stirring.
2 Flavour with vanilla and pour into a bowl or individual glasses. Sprinkle with a little sugar to prevent a skin forming. Serve with cream or whipped cream.

VARIATION
This dessert is excellent flavoured by the addition of a couple of tablespoons of orange marmalade or preserved, finely chopped orange peel with the vanilla.

Buttermilk Whip
(serves 4–5)
Preparation time: about 10 min
Unsuitable for the freezer

*1 egg
2 egg yolks
3–4 × 15ml tbsp (3–4tbsp) sugar
1 litre (1¾pt) buttermilk
½–1 lemon*

1 Whisk egg and egg yolks with

sugar until stiff. Transfer to a serving bowl.

2 Stir in ice cold buttermilk and flavour with juice and grated zest of lemon.

Serve with whipped cream and wafer thin lemon slices. Thin sugary biscuits go nicely with this.

VARIATION

Strawberry or Raspberry Whip
Replace lemon juice with fruit sprinkled with sugar and banana slices and chopped almonds sautéed in butter.

Creamed Rice

(serves 4–6)
Preparation time: 10 min
Unsuitable for the freezer

400–500ml (¾–1pt) rice pudding
several drops of vanilla essence
1 × 15ml tbsp (1tbsp) sugar (optional)
50ml (9fl oz) double cream

1 Sweeten pudding with vanilla and sugar, if liked.
2 Whip cream and mix well with pudding.
Serve with fruit sauce or jam.

On a hot summer's day choose cool Buttermilk Whip to serve as a dessert. This one is lemon flavoured.

45

A Classic Dessert

You do not have to be a Cordon Bleu cook to make this classic and ever-popular dessert. Simply follow the recipe and illustrations, step by step, and you can be guaranteed success.

Crème Caramel

1 Melt sugar in a heavy-based frying pan or saucepan. Do not stir until sugar is pale golden.

2 Pour caramel into mould(s). Hold mould(s) with thick oven gloves and turn to spread caramel evenly over the base of the mould.

Crème Caramel

(serves 5–6)
Preparation time: about 30 min
Cooking time: 25–60 min
Cooling time: 2–3 hr
Oven temperature (bottom shelf):
150°C, 300°F, Gas 2
Unsuitable for the freezer

350g (¾lb) sugar
5 eggs
500ml (1pt) single cream
½–1 vanilla pod
100–200ml (4–7fl oz) double cream

1 Melt about 225g (½lb) sugar in a dry frying pan on low to medium heat. Do not stir sugar until it starts to turn light brown and is bubbling along the edges of pan. Pour caramel into 5–6 warmed, ovenproof ramekins, into a large mould or a springform tin of about 1½ litres (2½pt) capacity.
2 Holding tins with thick oven gloves turn them quickly to allow the caramel to spread evenly. Pour any remaining mixture back into the frying pan, add about 200ml (7fl oz) hot water and boil, stirring, until the caramel has melted and the sauce is smooth. Pour into a jug and set aside to cool.
3 Beat eggs lightly with 100g (4oz) sugar. Bring cream to the boil with the vanilla pod then fold in egg mixture. Carefully strain into mould(s). Cover with foil and place in a roasting tin of boiling water.

4 Bake as indicated. Individual moulds will take 20–25 min, a ring mould 35–40 min and a large mould 45–60 min. Test with a skewer or sharp knife to check that the mixture has set.
5 Cool the crème caramel, turn out on serving dish while lukewarm and cool completely. Decorate with whipped cream and serve remaining caramel sauce separately, or stirred into whipped cream.

Caramel Cream Ring

(serves 6)
Preparation time: about 30 min
Setting time: 2–3 hr
Suitable for the freezer without caramel

15g (½oz) gelatine
50g (2oz) almonds
250g (9oz) granulated sugar
½ vanilla pod
50ml (2fl oz) single cream
3 eggs
4 × 15ml tbsp (4tbsp) caster sugar
250ml (9fl oz) double cream

1 Sprinkle gelatine over 3 × 15ml tbsp (3tbsp) water to soak. Blanch and chop almonds. Melt granulated sugar in a dry frying pan and pour half into a 1½ litre (2½pt) ring mould. Holding the tin with oven gloves turn it to allow caramel to spread evenly. Boil the remaining caramel in the frying pan with 150–200ml (5–7fl oz) water to give a smooth

sauce. Cool.
2 Bring single cream to the boil with chopped almonds and ½ split vanilla pod. Whisk egg yolks with sugar and whisk in some of the boiling cream. Pour back into the saucepan and cook, stirring constantly until smooth and thick, but do not allow to boil. Remove vanilla.
3 Dissolve gelatine over hot water then stir into the warm cream. Leave to set, stirring occasionally. When nearly set, fold in whisked egg whites and 100ml (4fl oz) whipped cream. Pour into a ring mould, cover with foil and leave to set.
4 Loosen the edges with a knife, dip the tin in hot water for a moment to allow the outer layer of caramel to melt, then turn out on to a serving dish.
5 Whip remaining cream. Stir in caramel sauce from frying pan and use this to fill the centre of the ring. Serve cold.

VARIATION
You can also make this dessert without putting the caramel into the mould – it is then easier to turn out. To serve, decorate with an almond brittle made from melted brown sugar mixed with 4–5 × 15ml tbsp (4–5tbsp) chopped almonds and a large pinch of baking powder. Pour this mixture onto greaseproof paper greased with oil, cool and crush with a rolling pin. Use this to fill the centre of the ring.

3 Bring cream to the boil with the vanilla and mix in whisked egg and sugar. Strain mixture and pour into mould(s).

4 Preheat the oven. Half-fill roasting tin with boiling water and place in the oven. Place mould(s) carefully in the water.

5 To test if pudding is done insert a sharp knife or skewer. It should come out clean. Remember that large moulds will need longer cooking time.

Pancakes and Waffles

Crêpes Suzette
(serves 4–5)
Preparation time: about 30 min
Cooling time: about 30 min
Pancakes are suitable for freezer without filling

For the pancakes:
100g (4oz) plain flour
½ × 5ml tsp (½tsp) salt
1 × 5ml tsp (1tsp) sugar
300ml (½pt) half or single cream
3 eggs
25g (1oz) butter
For the sauce:
25g (1oz) butter
2 oranges
8 sugar cubes
50ml (2fl oz) orange liqueur

1 Whisk together flour, salt, sugar, cream, eggs and melted butter to make a smooth batter. Fry thin pancakes and fold in four.
2 Put 25g (1oz) butter in a pan and place on a hotplate or over a spirit flame. Wash oranges well. Rub sugar cubes against orange peel until they disintegrate and fall into the pan. Squeeze the juice from oranges, pour into pan and bring to the boil.
3 Place pancakes in serving pan and heat in orange sauce. Add orange liqueur, heat through and set sauce alight with a match. Serve immediately, with soft vanilla ice cream if liked.

Apricot and Liqueur Cream Pancakes (left foreground)
(serves 8–10)
Preparation time: about 30 min
Cooking time: about 40 min
Suitable for the freezer without filling

For the pancakes (makes about 20)
250g (9oz) plain flour
4 large eggs
500ml (1pt) milk or buttermilk
1 × 5ml tsp (1tsp) salt
1 × 5ml tsp (1tsp) sugar
½ × 5ml tsp (½tsp) grated nutmeg
50g (2oz) butter
For the liqueur cream:
8g (¼oz) gelatine
3 egg yolks
3 × 15ml tbsp (3tbsp) icing sugar
1 × 5ml tsp (1tsp) vanilla essence
3 × 15ml tbsp (3tbsp) orange, apricot or peach liqueur
250ml (9fl oz) double cream
300ml (½pt) apricot purée
100g (4oz) almonds

1 Whisk together flour, eggs and about 200ml (7fl oz) milk or buttermilk to give a smooth batter. Add salt, sugar, nutmeg and remaining milk. Whisk well. Allow mixture to rest for about 15 min. Stir in melted butter.
2 Sprinkle gelatine over 2 × 15ml tbsp (2tbsp) cold water, soak, then dissolve over boiling water. Mix egg yolks with icing sugar and vanilla and stir in dissolved gelatine mixed with liqueur. When on the point of setting, fold in whipped cream.
3 Make medium sized, fairly thin pancakes. Blanch and flake almonds and grill until golden. Place a spoonful of liqueur cream and a spoonful of apricot purée on each pancake and roll up. Sprinkle with toasted almond flakes. Serve cold or warm.

Butter Waffles (left background)
(serves 4–6)
Preparation time: 15–20 min
Cooking time: about 30 min
Suitable for the freezer, but will lose a little of its flavour

For the waffle mixture:
125g (4½oz) self-raising flour
½ × 5ml tsp (½tsp) salt
1 × 5ml tsp (1tsp) caster sugar
2 large eggs
3 × 15ml tbsp (3tbsp) water
100ml (4fl oz) beer or non-alcoholic lager
100g (4oz) butter
100ml (4fl oz) double cream

1 Whisk together flour, salt, sugar, eggs, water and beer into a smooth batter. Melt butter, cool a little and whisk into mixture. Whip cream lightly and fold into mixture.
2 Heat waffle iron well on both sides. Teflon-coated ones need only be greased before making the first batch of waffles. Spoon 2–3 × 15ml tbsp (2–3tbsp) mixture onto iron, spread evenly, close the iron and turn over at once. Cook for 2–3 min, turn iron and cook for further 1–2 min. Remove waffle from iron using a fork and transfer to a wire rack. Serve waffles immediately with whipped cream and/or jam. You can also sprinkle them with sugar or icing sugar.

Frying pancakes
1 Put a knob of butter in a frying pan and ladle in some of the batter.

2 Turn pan quickly to allow batter to cover the surface in an even layer.

3 Pour off excess batter to ensure that pancakes are thin and even.

49

Cream Pancakes in Orange Sauce

(serves 4–5)
Preparation time: about 20 min
Resting time: 1 hr
Cooking time: about 20 min
Suitable for the freezer without sauce

For the pancakes:
3 eggs
4 × 15ml tbsp (4tbsp) plain flour
200ml (7fl oz) double cream
100ml (4fl oz) milk
1 × 5ml tsp (1tsp) sugar
50g (2oz) butter
1 × 5ml tsp (1tsp) vanilla essence or
* ½ grated vanilla pod*
1 × 5ml tsp (1tsp) grated lemon zest
For the sauce:
2 oranges
½–1 lemon
100g (4oz) butter
sugar to taste
2–3 × 15ml tbsp (2–3tbsp) Grand
* Marnier or other orange liqueur*

1 Whisk together flour, sugar, vanilla and grated lemon zest and stir in milk, cream, egg yolks and melted butter to make a smooth batter. Allow to rest for at least 1 hr. Just before cooking, fold in stiffly whisked egg whites.
2 Butter a frying pan or a small omelette or pancake pan and fry small, round pancakes until golden on both sides.
3 Mix orange and lemon juice, grated zest from ½ orange and ½ lemon, butter, sugar and liqueur in a shallow oven-to-table pan, bring to the boil then boil for a few minutes. Place saucepan over a spirit flame on the table and heat orange pancakes in the sauce. Serve warm with soured cream or soft vanilla ice cream.

Bread Crisps

(serves 4–6)
Preparation time: about 15 min
Unsuitable for the freezer

8 slices white bread
200ml (7fl oz) single cream
1 egg
cinnamon
sugar
butter for frying

1 Pour cream into a wide, fairly shallow dish and whisk in egg. Halve the bread slices and place in dish turning several times. When the bread has soaked up all the liquid (8–10 min) they are ready for frying.
2 Sprinkle slices on both sides with sugar and cinnamon and fry in batter until golden.
Serve with jam and/or cream.

VARIATION
Bread Crisps with Nuts
When bread slices have finished soaking, sprinkle with 100g (4oz) finely chopped nuts before frying. Sprinkle cooked slices with a little sugar and serve warm with apricot purée and soured cream.

Back : A variation of Bread Crisps sprinkled with chopped nuts.
Centre : Russian Pancake Stack – three thick pancakes layered with prune purée. Front : Cream Pancakes in Orange Sauce.

Yeast Waffles with Cheese Cream

(serves 4–6)
Preparation time: about 15 min
Rising time: about 30 min
Cooking time: about 30 min
Unsuitable for the freezer

For the batter :
15g (½oz) yeast
250ml (9fl oz) milk
½–1 × 5ml tsp (½–1tsp) salt
2 eggs
½ × 5ml tsp (½tsp) sugar
50g (2oz) butter
175g (6oz) plain flour
Cheese cream :
about 200g (7oz) full-fat soft cheese
1 egg yolk
2 lemons
milk

1 Dissolve yeast in about 100ml (4fl oz) lukewarm milk. Add the remaining milk, salt, eggs, sugar, flour and melted, cooled butter. Beat well and leave to rise in a warm place.
2 Heat waffle iron. If not Teflon-coated it should be greased. Spread 2–3 × 15ml tbsp (2–3tbsp) batter in iron, close and turn over at once. Cook for 2–3 min, turn again and cook for about 1 min. Remove waffle with a fork and place on a wire rack.
3 Soften cream cheese with a fork and beat with egg yolk, juice and finely grated zest of lemon and a little milk to make a smooth cheese cream.
4 Fill a piping bag fitted with a star nozzle with cheese cream. Separate waffles. Place 2 or 3 waffles together and pipe cheese cream between layers. Decorate with a rosette of cheese cream and a twist of lemon.

VARIATION
Yeast waffles can also be served with butter and cheese or other sandwich fillings.

Cream Waffles

(serves 4–6)
Preparation time: about 10 min
Cooking time: about 20 min
Unsuitable for the freezer

For the batter :
500ml (1pt) double cream
175g (6oz) self-raising flour
½–1 × 5ml tsp (½–1tsp) salt
1–2 × 5ml tsp (1–2tsp) sugar

1 Whip cream until nearly stiff and fold in sifted flour, salt and sugar.
2 Heat waffle iron thoroughly and if not Teflon-coated brush with butter.
3 Spread about 2 × 15ml tbsp (2tbsp) batter on iron, close and turn over at once. Cook for 2–3 min, turn iron and cook for 1–2 min more. Remove from grid with a fork and place on a wire rack. Cook remaining mixture in the same way.
Serve cream waffles warm, sprinkled with sugar or icing sugar. They also taste lovely with jam, whipped cream or vanilla ice cream.

TIP
Waffles can be heated through in an oven preheated to 200°C, 400°F, Gas 6, but do not pile them on top of each other or they will go soft.

Russian Pancake Stack

(serves 6–8)
Preparation time: about 20 min
Cooking time: about 45 min in all
Unsuitable for the freezer

For the batter :
100g (4oz) butter
250ml (9fl oz) water
250ml (9fl oz) double cream
5 eggs
125g (4½oz) plain flour
3 × 15ml tbsp (3tbsp) sugar
1 × 5ml tsp (1tsp) salt
1 × 15ml tbsp (1tbsp) grated lemon zest
50g (2oz) almonds
icing sugar
about 250g (9oz) prune purée or firm prune compote
butter for frying

1 Put butter, water and cream in a saucepan and bring to the boil. Sprinkle in flour and stir vigorously over medium heat until the mixture is shiny and leaves the sides of the pan. Leave to cool.
2 Beat in egg yolks, one at a time, beat in sugar, salt and grated lemon zest. Blanch and finely chop the almonds and add to mixture.
3 Whisk egg whites until standing in stiff peaks. Beat 2–3 egg whites into mixture and fold in the rest.
4 Melt the butter in a frying pan and spread ⅓ of the batter evenly in pan. Fry the pancake over fairly low heat for about 10 min. Butter a lid which fits frying pan and place over pan. Turn pancake onto lid and slide back into pan carefully. Bake pancake for about 5 min on other side.
5 Place cooked pancake on an oven-proof dish and keep warm in a very low oven. Fry 2 more pancakes and place the 3 pancakes together with prune purée or compote in between. Sift a little icing sugar on top.
Serve warm, sliced like a cake.

Lemon-flavoured Yeast Waffles with Cheese Cream are delicious after a light main course.

Orange Pancakes (below)

(serves 4–5)
Preparation time: about 25 min
Resting time for batter: 15 min
Cooking time: about 20 min
Suitable for freezer without filling

For the batter:
2 eggs
2 × 15ml tbsp (2tbsp) sugar
175g (6oz) plain flour
200ml (7fl oz) milk
50g (2oz) butter
1 orange
For the filling:
1 litre (1¾pt) vanilla ice cream
50g (2oz) almonds

1 Whisk eggs and sugar then whisk in flour, milk, melted butter and orange juice. Grate the orange zest finely and mix about 1 × 5ml tsp (1tsp) of this into mixture. Leave to rest for 15 min, stirring occasionally.
2 Blanch and chop almonds. Take ice cream out of freezer and place in refrigerator.
3 Fry fairly thin, medium-sized pancakes. Fold in 4 and place in a warm dish.
4 Slice ice cream and quickly tuck one slice inside each pancake. Sprinkle with almonds and the remaining grated orange peel. Serve immediately.

VARIATION

Instead of ice cream, fill the pancakes with whipped cream or soured cream then decorate in the same way.

Pancakes Alaska (Crêpes Alaska) (below right)

(serves 4)
Preparation time: about 30 min
Resting time for batter: about 30 min
Cooking time: about 20 min
Warming time: a few minutes
Oven temperature: 240°C, 475°F, Gas 9
Suitable for the freezer without filling

For the batter:
3 eggs
3 × 15ml tbsp (3tbsp) plain flour
200ml (7fl oz) single cream
¼ × 5ml tsp (¼tsp) salt
1 × 5ml tsp (1tsp) sugar
2–3 × 15ml tbsp (2–3tbsp) melted butter

For the filling:
½–¾ litre (1–1¾pt) vanilla ice cream
25–50g (1–2oz) almonds

1 Whisk eggs with flour, cream, salt, sugar and melted butter. Allow mixture to rest for 30 min. Fry thin, medium sized, pancakes and stack on a sheet of foil.
Pancakes can be made a day in advance.
2 Preheat oven. Blanch almonds and cut lengthways. Half fill an ovenproof dish with coarse salt. The salt acts as an insulator, prevents the ice cream melting too quickly, and makes the serving dish tolerate the difference in heat between the ice cold pancakes and the heat from the oven.
3 Remove ice cream from freezer – it should be solid. Slice with a knife dipped in warm water. Place one slice at the edge of each pancake, fold over sides and roll pancake around ice cream. Place the pancakes in a serving dish and sprinkle with almonds. Work quickly, so that the ice cream does not melt. Place in the oven and cook for 3–5 min.
Serve immediately, with a glass of champagne or fortified wine.

Liqueur Pancakes (right)
(serves 4–5)

Preparation time: about 30 min
Resting time for batter: 30 min
Cooking time: about 20 min
Unsuitable for the freezer

For the batter:
2 eggs
2 × 15ml tbsp (2tbsp) sugar
175g (6oz) plain flour
½ × 5ml tsp (½tsp) vanilla essence
150ml (¼pt) double cream
200–250ml (7–9fl oz) water
50–75g (2–3oz) melted butter
For the filling:
500–750g (1–1½lb) apples
juice of 1 orange
juice of ½ lemon
200ml (7fl oz) water
sugar
For the liqueur sauce:
50g (2oz) butter
juice of 1 orange
juice of ½ lemon
cooking syrup from apples
sugar to taste
50g (2oz) almonds
1–2 glasses liqueur

1 Whisk together eggs, sugar, flour, vanilla, cream, water and melted butter to a smooth, fairly thin batter. Allow to rest. Fry thin, small pancakes. They can be made a day in advance.

2 Make a syrup of orange and lemon juice, water and sugar to taste. Boil. Peel and core apples, and slice thinly. Poach apple slices in syrup until barely tender. Remove, then place apple slices on pancakes, roll up and arrange in an oven-to-table flameproof pan.

3 Mix cooking syrup with butter, orange and lemon juice, blanched flaked almonds and more sugar, if necessary. Bring sauce to the boil and pour over pancakes. Place pan on a stand over a spirit flame. Brown pancakes and pour over liqueur. Tilt pan slightly to set liqueur alight, and shake pan until the flames are extinguished. Always keep a lid handy to place over pan should the liqueur burn too long. Serve at once.

TIP
Instead of flambéeing, place pancakes in a flameproof dish, pour over sauce mixed with liqueur and bring to the boil. Heat in oven at 200°C, 400°F, Gas 6 for 5–8 min.

Hot Dessert Soufflés

Soufflé (basic recipe)
(serves 4–5)
Preparation time: about 20 min
Cooking time: about 30 min
(Individual dishes: 15–20 min)
Oven temperature (bottom shelf):
180–190°C, 350–375°F, Gas 4–5
Unsuitable for the freezer

25g (1oz) butter
25g (1oz) plain flour
250ml (9fl oz) milk or half cream
3 eggs
½ × 5ml tsp (½tsp) salt
1–3 × 5ml tsp (1–3tsp) sugar
flavouring, to taste

1 Melt butter in a saucepan over low heat. Stir in flour and cook for a minute or two, but do not allow to turn at all brown. Add milk, a little at a time, stirring all the time, to make a smooth sauce. Boil for 1–2 min, stirring. Cool.
2 Set oven at the correct temperature. Fold egg yolks into sauce, one at a time, stirring well between each addition. Stir in salt and sugar to taste and add vanilla, fruit juice, wine, liqueur or any other flavouring you choose.
3 Grease an ovenproof soufflé dish, capacity 1¼–1½ litres (2¼–2½pt). Whisk egg whites until standing in stiff peaks. Fold carefully into sauce, using a few quick strokes.
4 Pour soufflé mixture into prepared dish – it should not be more than ¾ full, and place in oven. Bake as indicated. Do not open oven door during cooking. Serve soufflé straight from oven, sprinkled with sifted icing sugar, if liked.
All hot soufflés will start to collapse the moment they are taken out of the oven. It is therefore sensible to let guests wait for the soufflé, not the other way round.

Left: Dessert soufflés should be light and airy. They can have fruit added, as shown here, or one of many other flavourings.
Right: Fluffy Soufflé Omelette, filled with cherries.

Soufflé Grand Marnier
Mix 2–3 × 15ml tbsp (2–3tbsp) Grand Marnier (or other liqueur) into soufflé before folding in the stiffly whisked egg whites: 2 × 15ml tbsp (2tbsp) sugar is sufficient in this recipe.

Fruit Soufflé
Place about 300g (11oz) lightly poached, fresh fruit or drained canned fruit without syrup at the bottom of the soufflé dish. Pour over soufflé mixture made using basic recipe.

Chocolate Soufflé
Add 1 × 15ml tbsp (1tbsp) cocoa powder, 2–3 × 15ml tbsp (2–3tbsp) icing sugar, 25g (1oz) blanched, chopped almonds and 50g (2oz) grated chocolate before folding in egg whites. Sift icing sugar over the top before serving.

Orange Soufflé
Use 3 × 5ml tsp (3tsp) sugar in mixture and add 2–3 × 15ml tbsp (2–3tbsp) orange juice and ½–1 × 15ml tbsp (½–1tbsp) finely grated orange zest to mixture before folding in egg whites. Canned mandarin oranges, peaches or other fruit can be used to form a base before pouring soufflé mixture over.

Lemon Soufflé
Use the same recipe as for Orange Soufflé, but use lemon juice and grated lemon zest.

All these suggestions for various dessert soufflées can also be used for soufflé omelettes.

Soufflé Omelette
(serves 2–3)
Preparation time: 15–20 min
Cooking time: 5–8 min
Unsuitable for the freezer

3 eggs
1 × 5ml tsp (1tsp) icing sugar
4–5 × 15ml tbsp (4–5tbsp) double
  cream
½ × 5ml tsp (½tsp) vanilla essence
8–10 almonds
butter for frying
  fruit filling to taste
icing sugar

1 Separate eggs and whisk whites until standing in stiff peaks. Whisk egg yolks lightly with icing sugar, cream, vanilla and blanched, finely chopped almonds. Fold carefully into egg whites.
2 Put 25–40g (1–1½oz) butter in a medium sized frying pan and heat until pale brown in colour. Pour in egg mixture and fry omelette over low heat. Shake the pan and make a few holes in the mixture with a spatula so that egg mixture runs to the bottom of the pan.
3 The omelette is ready when the bottom is firm and leaves the pan easily, and the surface is frothy.
Slide omelette onto a hot serving dish. Place warm fruit, compote or jam on one half and fold the other half over. Sift icing sugar over top.

Suggestion for filling:
Sprinkle 1–2 × 15ml tbsp (1–2tbsp) sugar over 150–200g (5–7oz) sweet cherries. Sprinkle with 1–2 × 15ml tbsp (1–2tbsp) cherry brandy and heat through carefully.

Ice Cream

The favourite dessert for children and adults alike, ice cream comes in many guises — from simple vanilla to a party dessert with nuts, chocolate or fruit.
Use these basic recipes for both creamed ice and ice with whipped cream on which there are countless variations.

Cream Ice (Parfait)

(Serves 4–6)
Preparation time: 15–20 min
Freezing time: about 3 hr

4 egg yolks
3 × 15ml tbsp (3tbsp) sugar
½ × 5ml tsp (½tsp) vanilla essence
2 egg whites
500ml (1pt) double cream

1 Whisk egg yolks and sugar until thick. Add vanilla essence.
2 Whisk egg whites until standing in stiff peaks. Whip cream and mix with the egg whites into the yolks. Use a soft rubber spatula, and work upwards from the bottom of the bowl, to mix all the ingredients thoroughly.
3 Rinse out a tin of capacity about 1½ litres (2½pt) with cold water. Add egg mixture and cover tightly with a lid or foil. Freeze at a temperature of −18°C (0°F) for about 3 hr. Do not stir ice cream while it is in the freezer. Remove from freezer and transfer to the refrigerator for 15 min before serving.

Whipped Cream Ice

(serves 4–6)
Preparation time: 20–25 min
Cooling time: about 1 hr
Freezing time: about 3 hr

250ml (9fl oz) water
½ vanilla pod
250ml (9fl oz) double cream
3 egg yolks
85g (3½oz) sugar
½ × 5ml tsp (½tsp) gelatine

1 Sprinkle gelatine over a little cold water. Slice open vanilla pod, put in a saucepan with water and bring to the boil. Add cream. Whisk egg yolks and sugar until stiff. Pour some of the boiling cream mixture onto egg yolks, whisk vigorously. Pour back into saucepan set over low heat.
2 Whip mixture vigorously until cream thickens, but do not allow to boil. Remove vanilla pod. Dissolve gelatine over boiling water then stir into cream. Remove from the heat and cool, whisking occasionally.
3 Pour mixture into a tin or bowl and cover lightly with a lid or foil. Freeze at −18°C (0°F) or cooler. Remove ice cream after about 1½ hr, stir well and replace in freezer. This

ice cream is soft in consistency. Whipped Cream Ice can, like Cream Ice, be given added interest by the use of a variety of additional flavourings.

Almond Brittle Ice

(serves 4–6)
Preparation time: about 20 min
Freezing time: about 3 hr

1 quantity Cream Ice
175g (6oz) sugar
50g (2oz) almonds or other nuts

1 Blanch almonds and chop coarsely. For other nuts, rub off skins before chopping.
2 Melt sugar in a dry frying pan over moderate heat. When the sugar is golden, add chopped nuts. Stir sugar mixture for a moment and pour onto greased greaseproof paper.
3 When cold, crush the almond brittle with a rolling pin and stir into ice cream with egg whites and cream. Freeze as in basic recipe.
Serve with a rosette of whipped cream and toasted almond flakes.

Mocha Walnut Ice Cream

(serves 4–6)
Preparation time: about 20 min
Freezing time: about 3 hr

1 quantity Whipped Cream Ice
3 × 15ml tbsp (3tbsp) instant coffee
50g (2oz) walnuts
4–5 × 15ml tbsp (4–5tbsp) sugar
2 egg whites
100ml (4fl oz) double cream

1 Make Whipped Cream Ice (see basic recipe), but add instant coffee to water instead of vanilla pod.
2 Melt sugar in a dry frying pan and heat until lightly golden. Place 4–6 undamaged walnut halves in pan, turn until covered with caramel and place on oiled greaseproof paper. Remove pan from heat, chop remaining nuts and stir into caramel with 50–100ml (2–4fl oz) boiling water. Stir until mixture is smooth and thick but still flowing. Stir into cream mixture.
3 Whisk egg whites until standing in stiff peaks and fold into the chilled cream mixture. Freeze as indicated, stirring after ½ hr in freezer and again after 1½ hr. Serve ice icream in sundae glasses and decorate with

whipped cream and caramelized walnuts. Serve immediately.

Liqueur Ice Cream
(serves 4–6)
Preparation time: about 20 min
Freezing time: about 3 hr

1 quantity Cream Ice
4 × 15ml tbsp (4tbsp) Grand Marnier, Tia Maria, Drambuie or other liqueur
2 × 15ml tbsp (2tbsp) coffee beans or instant coffee
40–50g (1½–2oz) cooking chocolate

1 Mix 2 × 15ml tbsp (2tbsp) liqueur into cream mixture just before freezing. Crush the whole coffee beans, put in a plastic bag and crush more finely with a rolling pin. Grate cooking chocolate.
2 Spoon ice cream into large deep glasses and sprinkle with remaining liqueur. Sprinkle with crushed coffee beans or instant coffee, mixed with grated chocolate. Serve at once.

Ice Delight
(serves 6)
Preparation time: about 30 min
Freezing time: about 3 hr

1 almond base (see page 21)
1 quantity Cream Ice or Almond Brittle Ice
50g (2oz) walnuts
100g (4oz) cooking chocolate
50g (2oz) maraschino cherries

1 Bake an almond base following recipe given for Rubenstein Gâteau (page 21).
2 Set aside 6–8 walnut halves and a small piece of chocolate. Chop the remaining chocolate and nuts coarsely. Chop cherries. Fold nuts, chocolate and cherries into ice cream just before freezing.
3 Turn out the finished ice cream onto almond base and decorate with grated chocolate and walnut halves. Serve immediately.

Left: Mocha Walnut Ice Cream is an ice cream for adult palates.
Above right: Liqueur Ice Cream.
Right: Almond Brittle Ice on an almond base.

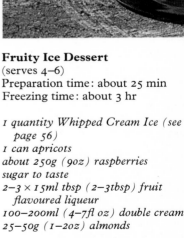

Blackcurrant Ice Cream
(serves 4–6)
Preparation time: about 20 min
Freezing time: about 3 hr

1 quantity Cream Ice (see page 56)
150–250g (5–9oz) ripe
  blackcurrants
5–6 × 15ml tbsp (5–6tbsp) sugar
2 × 15ml tbsp (2tbsp) blackcurrant
  cordial or liqueur (Crème de
  Cassis)
100–200ml (4–7fl oz) double cream

1 Make ice cream following basic
recipe and put in freezer. Rinse and
clean blackcurrants and mix with
sugar and cordial or liqueur. Allow

to stand for 10–15 min.
2 Remove ice cream from freezer
20–30 min before serving and place
in refrigerator. Spoon ice cream into
individual glasses, in layers with
sugar syrup from blackcurrants.
Spoon blackcurrants over ice cream
and decorate with cream. Serve at
once, with Pompadour wafers or
small, crisp macaroons.

VARIATION
You can also use other juicy soft
fruit in this dessert, including strawberries, raspberries, redcurrants,
and cherries. Add sugar to taste and
marinate fruit in sherry, madeira or
port.

Fruity Ice Dessert
(serves 4–6)
Preparation time: about 25 min
Freezing time: about 3 hr

1 quantity Whipped Cream Ice (see
  page 56)
1 can apricots
about 250g (9oz) raspberries
sugar to taste
2–3 × 15ml tbsp (2–3tbsp) fruit
  flavoured liqueur
100–200ml (4–7fl oz) double cream
25–50g (1–2oz) almonds

1 Make Whipped Cream Ice following basic recipe and put in the
freezer. Drain apricots well. Rinse

raspberries if necessary, sprinkle with sugar and finally with fruit flavoured liqueur.

2 Whip cream. Blanch and halve almonds.

3 Arrange Whipped Cream Ice in layers with apricots and strawberries in tall individual glasses and sprinkle with liqueur syrup. Decorate with lightly whipped cream and blanched almonds. Serve immediately.

Ice Cream with Chocolate Pears

(serves 4–6)
Preparation time: about 30 min
Freezing time: about 3 hr

1 quantity Whipped Cream Ice (see page 56)
6 ripe pears
175g (6oz) sugar
1 glass white wine or juice of 1 lemon
For the chocolate sauce:
100ml (4fl oz) water
150g (5oz) cooking chocolate
15g (½oz) butter
3 × 15ml tbsp (3tbsp) double cream

1 Make Whipped Cream Ice and place in freezer. Make a syrup with sugar, 200ml (7fl oz) water and white wine or lemon juice. Peel pears. Remove eye but leave stalk intact. Remove the core, if liked, making a hole through the pear from the eye end, but make sure pears stay whole.

2 Scrape pear stalks with a sharp knife and boil pears until nearly tender in sugar syrup. Cool in syrup.

3 Break chocolate into small pieces and melt in water in a heavy-based saucepan. When chocolate is smooth, carefully whisk in butter and cream.

4 Spoon ice into wide individual glasses or dishes. Place a pear in the middle of each glass and pour over some of the warm chocolate sauce. Serve at once with the remaining chocolate sauce handed separately and with almond macaroons or cigar-shaped biscuits.

Melon Ice Dessert
(serves 4–6)
Preparation time: about 30 min
Freezing time: about 3 hr

1 small honeydew melon
½–1 litre (1–1¾pt) Cream Ice
 or ready-made vanilla ice cream
2–3 × 15ml tbsp (2–3tbsp) port
50g (2oz) almonds
200ml (7fl oz) double cream

1 Make Cream Ice using basic recipe (page 56) and place in the freezer. Chill melon in refrigerator for 2 hr.
2 Cut melon into wedges and remove seeds. Scoop out balls of melon flesh with a melon baller, cover skins and flesh tightly and refrigerate. Blanch and coarsely chop almonds and colour with artificial colouring if liked.
3 Pile crushed ice onto individual serving plates and place scooped melon wedges on top. Sprinkle with port. Shape balls of ice cream with ice cream scoop or use 2 rounded tablespoons dipped in water.
Place ice cream and melon balls in melon wedges. Decorate with cream and chopped almonds. Serve immediately.

Ice Cream Sundaes

Make these delicious ice cream sundaes, based on either shop bought or homemade ice cream using the recipes on page 56. If you do not have time to make your own ice cream, a ready-made, good quality variety mixed with fruit, fruit juice, wine or liqueur will be nearly as good as homemade.
Always remember to wait until just before serving to add fruit.

Fruit Salad Sundae

(serves 4–6)
Preparation time: about 30 min
Freezing time: about 3 hr
Marinating time: 20–30 min

1 quantity Cream Ice or Whipped
Cream Ice or, if liked, make up in
several smaller portions flavoured
with apricot, strawberry or peach
(you can also use ready-made
vanilla ice cream flavoured in the
same way)
2 oranges
4 kiwi fruits
250g (9oz) strawberries
2–3 bananas
1 small bunch of black grapes
sugar to taste
3 × 15ml tbsp (3tbsp) white rum
250ml (9fl oz) double cream
25–50g (1–2oz) almonds

1 Make up Cream Ice or Whipped
Cream Ice (see page 56) with additional flavourings if liked, and
place in freezer.
2 Clean and chop fruit. Sprinkle
with sugar to taste, then sprinkle
with rum and leave to marinate as
indicated.
3 Whip cream and spoon into a
piping bag. Blanch and chop or flake

almonds, then toast until golden
under the grill.
4 Spoon fruit, including marinade,
into chilled individual glasses.
Shape the ice cream into balls with
an ice cream scoop and place on top.
Decorate with cream, almonds and
semi-sweet biscuits. Serve at once.

Florentine Ice Cream Sundae

(serves 4–6)
Preparation time: about 30 min
Freezing time: about 3 hr

½ quantity Cream Ice or Almond
Brittle Ice (see page 56)
½ quantity coffee- or chocolate-
flavoured Whipped Cream Ice or
similar ready-made ice cream
about 50g (2oz) Rice Krispies
250ml (9fl oz) double cream
50–75g (2–3oz) hazelnuts
8–10 small Florentines

1 Place ice cream in freezer. Rub
skins off hazelnuts and chop
coarsely.
2 Spoon the ice cream into tall individual glasses in layers with Rice
Krispies.
Whip cream and pipe small rosettes
onto ice cream. Decorate with nut
kernels and Florentines.

Cherry Sorbet Special

(serves 4–6)
Preparation time: 20–25 min
Freezing time: 5 hr

Sorbet : 400ml (¾pt) cherry brandy
300–400ml (½–¾pt) soda water
½ quantity Cream Ice
200ml (7fl oz) double cream
100g (4oz) fresh, sweet cherries

1 Mix cherry brandy and soda
water and freeze for about 5 hr in a
freezer container with tightly fitting
lid. Stir well after 2 hr in freezer and
again at ½–1 hr intervals. Make
Cream Ice and freeze. Whip cream
lightly and rinse cherries.
2 Remove sorbet and stir carefully.
Layer sorbet and cream ice in chilled glasses. Decorate with lightly
whipped cream and cherries.
Serve immediately.

Far left : Melon Ice Dessert.
Below left : Fruit Salad Sundae.
Below right : Florentine Ice Cream
Sundae.

Cheese to Follow

Cheese is always a fitting end to a meal, unless it has featured strongly in the main course. Rather than serving an ordinary cheeseboard, why not try some of these interesting ways with cheese?

Cheese Mousse
(serves 6–8)
Preparation time: 20–30 min
Setting time: about 2 hr
Unsuitable for the freezer

8g (¼oz) gelatine
200g (7oz) Gorgonzola or other blue cheese
200g (7oz) natural cream cheese
250ml (9fl oz) double cream
2–3 × 15ml tbsp (2–3tbsp) brandy
paprika
walnut halves
black grapes

Left : Cheese Mousse, decorated with walnut halves and black grapes. Below right : If you bake the pastry for this Cheese Cake in advance, it can quickly be filled with cheese cream.

1 Sprinkle gelatine over 2 × 15ml tbsp (2tbsp) cold water and soak for 5 min. Dissolve over a saucepan of boiling water. Mash blue cheese and cream cheese with a fork, then beat together until smooth. Pour brandy into the dissolved gelatine and stir into the cheese mixture. Season with paprika. Fold in whipped cream.

2 Rinse out a 1 litre (1¾pt) mould with cold water and spoon in cheese mixture. Cover with foil and leave in a cold place for 2 hr or overnight. Turn mousse out onto a serving dish and decorate with walnut halves and black grapes.

Serve with toast and/or biscuits and butter.

Cheese Cake

(serves 6–8)
Preparation time: about 30 min
Cooking time: 10–12 min
Oven temperature (middle shelf):
200°C, 400°F, Gas 6
Suitable for the freezer without decoration

For the pastry :
200g (7oz) plain flour
200g (7oz) butter
50ml (2fl oz) water
For the cheese cream :
300ml (½pt) single cream
4 × 15ml tbsp (4tbsp) plain flour
3 small eggs
100g (4oz) mild cheese, grated
50g (2oz) Parmesan cheese, grated
200–250g (7–9oz) softened butter
To decorate :
25g (1oz) walnuts
50–75g (2–3oz) stuffed olives
radishes

1 Rub butter into flour, add water and quickly draw mixture together. Leave pastry in a cold place for 1–2 hr or overnight. (It will keep for about 1 week in the refrigerator.)

2 Divide pastry into 3 and roll into circles, each about 22cm (8½in) in diameter. Place circles on well greased baking sheets and bake as indicated. Transfer to a smooth surface to cool. The baked pastry can be kept for several days in an airtight tin.

3 Remove butter for cheese cream from the refrigerator well in advance. It should be soft before use. Work together a paste of flour and cream, bring to the boil, stirring, and cool. Whisk in eggs, one at a time, then stir in the grated cheese. Add softened butter, a little at a time, whisking until the mixture is smooth.

4 Sandwich pastry rounds together with most of the cream. Smooth a thin layer of cheese cream over the top and pipe the remainder in small rosettes around the edge. Decorate with olives, walnuts and radishes. Chill.

Serve cut into wedges.

VARIATION

Flavour the cheese cream with 2–3 × 15ml tbsp (2–3tbsp) port and finely chopped walnuts or dry sherry and paprika. Do not use grapes as a decoration. They do not go well with olives and radishes.

Deep Fried Camembert

(serves 4–6)
Preparation time: about 10 min
Cooking time: a few minutes
Unsuitable for the freezer

4–6 small Camembert triangles
1 egg
breadcrumbs
oil or lard

1 Use hard, unripe Camembert and refrigerate until you are ready to use it. Heat oil or fat in a chip pan.

2 Coat cheese with beaten egg then with breadcrumbs. Set aside to allow coating to dry.

3 Lower cheese pieces into the oil 2 or 3 at a time, then turn them with a slotted spoon until they are golden brown all over. Drain on absorbent paper.

Serve hot with blackcurrant or cherry jam or with celery.

TIP

Coated, but not fried Camembert can be frozen and will keep for 1–2 months. Wrap each piece separately. Fry from frozen for 2 min longer than recommended and at a lower temperature. Frozen or unfrozen cheese can also be fried in butter in frying pan.

Index